The Civil War:
The Fall of the Confederacy and the End of Slavery

The Civil War:
The Fall of the Confederacy and the End of Slavery

Titles in the History's Great Defeats series include:

HISTORY'S GREAT DEFEATS

The Civil War:
The Fall of the Confederacy and the End of Slavery

by Richard Brownell

LUCENT BOOKS

An imprint of Thomson Gale, a part of The Thomson Corporation

THOMSON
™
GALE

Detroit • New York • San Francisco • San Diego • New Haven, Conn.
Waterville, Maine • London • Munich

THOMSON

---*---™

GALE

© 2005 Thomson Gale, a part of The Thomson Corporation.

Thomson and Star Logo are trademarks and Gale and Lucent Books are registered trademarks used herein under license.

For more information, contact
Lucent Books
27500 Drake Rd.
Farmington Hills, MI 48331-3535
Or you can visit our Internet site at http://www.gale.com

LIBRARY OF CONGRESS CATALOGING-IN-PUBLICATION DATA

Brownell, Richard.
    The Civil War: The fall of the Confederacy and the end of slavery / By Richard Brownell.
      p. cm. -- (History's great defeats)
    Includes bibliographical references and index.
    ISBN 1-59018-429-7 (alk. paper)
1. Confederate States of America--Politics and government--Juvenile literature. 2. Slavery--Southern States--History--19th century--Juvenile literature. 3. Confederate States of America--Social conditions--Juvenile literature. 4. Confederate States of America--Economic conditions--Juvenile literature. 5. United States--Politics and government--1861-1865--Juvenile literature. 6. United States--History--Civil War, 1861-1865--Juvenile literature. I. Title. II. Series.
    E487.B756 2005
    973.7'13--dc22

                                      2004011909

Printed in the United States of America

Table of Contents

Foreword

HISTORY IS FILLED with tales of dramatic encounters that sealed the fates of empires or civilizations, changing them or causing them to disappear forever. One of the best known events began in 334 B.C., when Alexander, king of Macedonia, led his small but formidable Greek army into Asia. In the short span of only ten years, he brought Persia, the largest empire the world had yet seen, to its knees, earning him the nickname forever after associated with his name—"the Great." The demise of Persia, which at its height stretched from the shores of the Mediterranean Sea in the west to the borders of India in the east, was one of history's most stunning defeats. It occurred primarily because of some fatal flaws in the Persian military system, disadvantages the Greeks had exploited before, though never as spectacularly as they did under Alexander.

First, though the Persians had managed to conquer many peoples and bring huge territories under their control, they had failed to create an individual fighting man who could compare with the Greek hoplite. A heavily armored infantry soldier, the hoplite fought in a highly effective and lethal battlefield formation—the phalanx. Possessed of better armor, weapons, and training than the Persians, Alexander's soldiers repeatedly crushed their Persian opponents. Second, the Persians for the most part lacked generals of the caliber of their Greek counterparts. And when Alexander invaded, Persia had the added and decisive disadvantage of facing one of the greatest generals of all time. When the Persians were defeated, their great empire was lost forever.

Other world powers and civilizations have fallen in a like manner. They have succumbed to some combination of inherent fatal flaws or disadvantages, to political and/or military mistakes, and even to the personal failings of their leaders.

Another of history's great defeats was the sad demise of the North American Indian tribes at the hands of encroaching European civilization from the sixteenth to nineteenth centuries. In this case, all of the tribes suffered from the same crippling disadvantages. Among the worst, they lacked the great numbers, the unity, and the advanced industrial and military hardware possessed by the Europeans. Still another example, one closer to our own time, was the resounding defeat of Nazi Germany by the Allies in 1945, which brought World War II, the most disastrous conflict in history, to a close. Nazi Germany collapsed for many reasons. But one of the most telling was that its leader, Adolf Hitler, sorely underestimated the material resources and human resolve of the Allies, especially the United States. In the end, Germany was in a very real sense submerged by a massive and seemingly relentless tidal wave of Allied bombs, tanks, ships, and soldiers.

Seen in retrospect, a good many of the fatal flaws, drawbacks, and mistakes that caused these and other great defeats from the pages of history seem obvious. It is only natural to wonder why, in each case, the losers did not realize their limitations and/or errors sooner and attempt to avert disaster. But closer examination of the events, social and political trends, and leading personalities involved usually reveals that complex factors were at play. Arrogance, fear, ignorance, stubbornness, innocence, and other attitudes held by nations, peoples, and individuals often colored and shaped their reactions, goals, and strategies. And it is both fascinating and instructive to reconstruct how such attitudes, as well as the fatal flaws and mistakes themselves, contributed to the losers' ultimate demise.

Each volume in Lucent Books' *History's Great Defeats* series is designed to provide the reader with diverse learning tools for exploring the topic at hand. Each well-informed, clearly written text is supported and enlivened by substantial quotes by the actual people involved, as well as by later historians and other experts; and these primary and secondary sources are carefully documented. Each volume also supplies the reader with an extensive Works Consulted list, guiding him or her to further research on the topic. These and other research tools, including glossaries and time lines, afford the reader a thorough understanding of how and why one of history's most decisive defeats occurred and how these events shaped our world.

Moving Toward Conflict

Introduction

There will never again be harmony between the two great sections of the Union.

Alexander H. Stephens, quoted in
The Union That Shaped the Confederacy
by William C. Davis

PERHAPS NO ISSUE more consumed America's leaders during the first half of the nineteenth century than slavery. Virtually no action on the part of the federal government was taken without some consideration of how it might affect the balance of power between the slaveholding states of the South and the non-slaveholding North. Particularly as the nation expanded and new states sought entry to the Union, the controversy over what one of America's founders, Thomas Jefferson, had referred to as the Peculiar Institution, raged. While the North sought to contain slavery in areas where it already existed, hoping that it would eventually fade into history, the South sought the expansion of territory where slavery was legal.

Pushing the Slavery Agenda

Southerners believed that the right to own slaves—who they considered as personal property—was guaranteed by the Constitution, and any restriction of it was a violation of states' rights. The growing abolition movement in the North, with its strong support from Northern politicians, made the South progressively more fearful that Congress would someday ban slavery altogether. That fear unified the South, despite a long-held devotion to the idea that individual states' rights were of paramount importance. South Carolina senator John C. Calhoun told his fellow Southern legislators in 1836, "We are here but a handful in the midst of an overwhelming majority. It is the duty of every member from the South . . . to avoid everything calculated to divide and distract our ranks."[1] On the floor of the House and Senate, Southern congressmen attempted to prevent open discussion of slavery using the "gag" rule. The preamble of the document in which this rule was articulated stated, "It is extremely important and desirable that the agitation of this subject should be finally arrested, for the purpose of restoring tranquility to the public mind."[2]

Attempts at Compromise

The question of whether to permit slavery in states that were yet to be admitted to the Union could not be avoided. The first attempt to settle the slavery issue was the Missouri Compromise of 1820, which prohibited slavery above latitude 36° 30' north in the lands that had been acquired from France in the Louisiana Purchase in 1803. This measure was

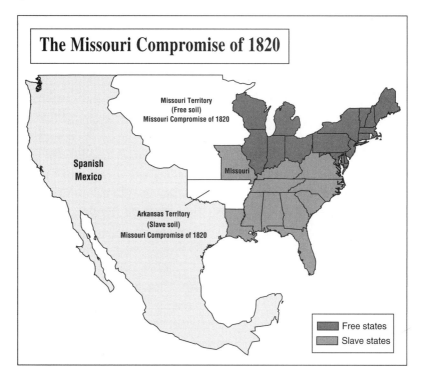

The Missouri Compromise of 1820

Missouri Territory
(Free soil)
Missouri Compromise of 1820

Spanish
Mexico

Missouri

Arkansas Territory
(Slave soil)
Missouri Compromise of 1820

Free states
Slave states

designed to maintain the balance of power between the free states of the North and the slave states of the South.

The Missouri Compromise was only a temporary solution. Whenever new states sought admission the balance was threatened. The issue of slave versus free states became even more inflamed in the aftermath of the Mexican War, which had resulted in Mexico ceding an enormous swath of territory to the United States. Eventually, another accommodation was reached. Known as the Compromise of 1850, this package of laws allowed California to enter the Union as a free state. Additionally, other states that would in the future be carved from the territory won from Mexico were allowed to decide for themselves whether or not to accept slavery, a concept known as popular sovereignty.

The idea of letting voters decide the slavery question soon led to violence. In 1854, Illinois senator Stephen Douglas proposed carving two states from the vast Nebraska Territory, a large expanse of land that had been part of the Louisiana Purchase. The Kansas-Nebraska Act that Douglas crafted allowed for settling the slavery issue in the territories by popular sovereignty. As the prospect of statehood loomed, both slave and abolitionist forces moved into Kansas intent on swaying the popular vote. Mob violence broke out across the territory as armed zealots on both sides tried to intimidate voters and force them to vote one way or the other or simply not to vote at all.

A Violent Mood

The violent mood affecting the nation was evident even in Congress. In one notorious incident, South Carolina congressman Preston Brooks beat Massachusetts senator Charles Sumner nearly to death for Sumner's antislavery remarks. Brooks's Southern colleagues, like Robert Toombs of Georgia, treated the incident casually. "Yankees seem greatly excited about Sumner's flogging," Toombs said. "They are afraid the practice may become general."[3]

Just as congressional action failed to settle the slavery question, so too did the Supreme Court fail to end the dispute. In 1857 the Supreme Court affirmed the Southern argument that slaves were property protected by the Constitution in the *Dred Scott v. Sandford* case, noting that a slave did not become free simply by entering a nonslave state. In Chief Justice Roger Taney's opinion, the Missouri Compromise was unconstitutional because "an act of Congress which deprives

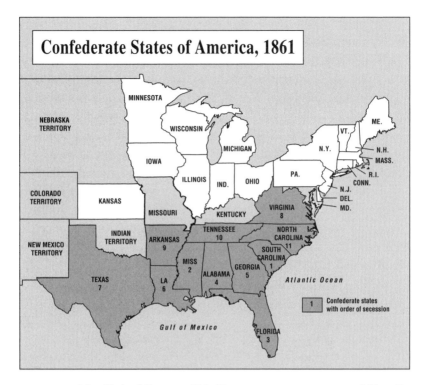

Confederate States of America, 1861

a person of the United States of his liberty or property . . . could hardly be dignified with the name of due process of law."[4] By extension, any restriction on slavery was similarly unconstitutional.

Southerners found little solace in the *Dred Scott* decision. When Abraham Lincoln was elected president in 1860, the South believed that he would soon act to forcibly end slavery. Lincoln tried to reassure Southerners, stating in his inauguration speech, "I have no purpose, directly or indirectly, to interfere with the institution of slavery in the states where it exists. I believe I have no lawful right to do so, and I have no inclination to do so."[5] Lincoln's assertions made no difference. Seven states had already seceded from the Union and formed the Confederate States of America.

The new nation moved swiftly to seize Union property within its borders, including, among other installations, Fort Sumter, which lay in South Carolina's Charleston Harbor. Lincoln announced his intentions to supply the besieged garrison with much-needed nonmilitary provisions. Confederate president Jefferson Davis was placed in a difficult position—either be seen as backing down on his threats to attack

Fort Sumter or be forced to fire the first shot of a war, a shot fired to prevent food from reaching hungry men.

Confederate secretary of state Toombs advised against attack. "You will lose us every friend at the North. . . . It is unnecessary. It puts us in the wrong. It is fatal."[6] Davis ignored Toombs's pleas and issued an ultimatum to the Union force, which was turned down. Fort Sumter was fired upon April 12, 1861, and surrendered two days later.

The next day Lincoln issued a call for seventy-five thousand volunteers to enlist and force the rebels to rejoin the Union. Northerners in general were outraged over Fort Sumter, as Toombs predicted, and eagerly rallied behind their president. Secessionists in Virginia, Arkansas, North Carolina, and Tennessee, their position hardened by Lincoln's call for soldiers, joined the Confederacy. The war that some had predicted and many hoped never to see had begun.

Chapter 1

War Between the States: A Battle of Wills

Morale was the most potent weapon the South had; and with all the Confederates' uncoordinated efforts at building it up and maintaining it, they lost this weapon, and, therefore, the war.

E. Merton Coulter, *The Confederate States of America, 1861–1865*

EVEN AFTER THE attack on Fort Sumter and the secession of the Southern states made war inevitable, in early 1861 neither the North nor the South was prepared for an armed struggle. Just the same, in terms of possessing the ability to prosecute a war, the Union maintained certain undeniable advantages over the South, chiefly its much larger population and more vigorous industrial base. Before resigning as superintendent of the Louisiana State Military Academy to return to his native Ohio, William Tecumseh Sherman told a Southern friend in December 1860, "Only in your spirit and determination are you prepared for war. In all else you are totally unprepared."[7]

In this, Sherman was right. Morale was the most important asset the fledgling Confederacy possessed, but this alone could not win the war for the South. Extended conflict with a Union army that enjoyed superior numbers and equipment brought brutal hardship to Confederate soldiers and civilians alike, wearing down both their ability to fight and their will to carry on the war.

Beginnings: A War of Mutual Disadvantage

At first, it seemed that the two sides faced similar liabilities. Both the Union and the Confederacy entered hostilities with new national leaders who shouldered the burden of putting together presidential administrations during a rapidly escalating crisis. Lincoln's task was not made easier by the rocky relations between him and Congress, where many members thought him to be well-meaning but incompetent. Even his own Republican Party, far from a unified organization, had little faith in him. This was demonstrated in Lincoln's cabinet, where the secretaries were given to infighting and mistrust of each other and a lack of faith in the president. Secretary of the Navy Gideon Welles, for example, often complained that Lincoln's administrative abilities were inadequate. Lincoln kept an irregular schedule that meant infrequent cabinet meetings, but he worked long hours and, as Pulitzer Prize–winning biographer David Herbert Donald notes, his "systematic lack of system seemed to work."[8]

During the Civil War, Abraham Lincoln (left), a man of limited political experience, served as president of the Union, while Jefferson Davis, a seasoned politician, led the Confederacy.

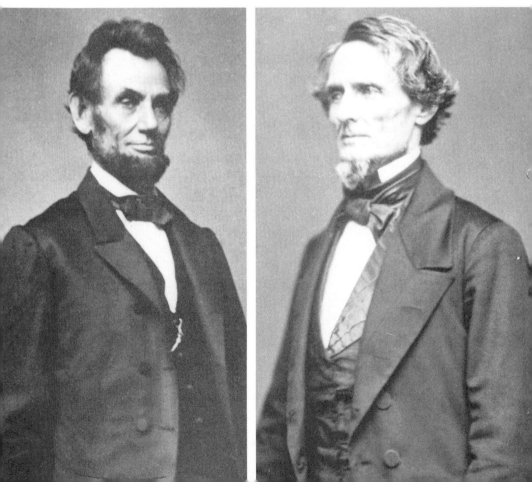

Still, while Lincoln needed to construct an efficient administration, Confederate president Jefferson Davis needed to establish an entire nation from the ground up, and he may have been better suited to the task at hand than his Northern counterpart. While Lincoln's government experience amounted to only one term in the House of Representatives and two failed bids for the Senate, Davis had been a distinguished member of the Senate before secession and had served as secretary of war under President Franklin Pierce. As a West Point graduate and a hero of the Battle of Buena Vista during the Mexican War, Davis had military experience greater than any other member of his administration.

One of Davis's first command decisions was to create an army, and in March 1861 he called for one hundred thousand volunteers. He then sought fellow West Point graduates of professional caliber like P.G.T. Beauregard, Joseph E. Johnston, and Robert E. Lee to lead them. Davis's opponents in certain states considered this an exercise in crony patronage, but would unabashedly submit names of their own for officer assignments, seeking men to represent their home states without regard for their capabilities.

The Union was also in need of a conditioned fighting force and a command to lead them. After Lincoln called for volunteers, he created a command structure to take charge of the thousands of men that each state offered. Much of the first half of the war for the Union was a process of trial-and-error military appointments, and those who proved inefficient or who opposed Lincoln's strategy were replaced.

If leading the Union men in battle was a problem, arming them was not. Lincoln assumed unprecedented sweeping powers in order to prosecute the war, converting the North's heavy industrial capacity over to wartime manufacturing. He also had the power to borrow money for financing military procurement and established a national banking system and currency to help pay for what the Union needed.

The Confederate government similarly stepped in to regulate industry, encouraging the manufacturing of weapons and goods for the army, but arming its soldiers proved more difficult than it did in the North. A significantly smaller industrial base meant fewer factories for producing rifles, and the guns that militias did possess were the property of the state governments, which were reluctant to let these precious weapons leave their control.

A War of Numbers

When it came to the men who would carry those weapons, the South was also at a disadvantage. According to the 1860 U.S. census, the population of the country stood at 31,443,321. The eleven states of the Confederacy comprised approximately 9 million of that number, with close to 4 million being slaves. Of white males aged fifteen to forty—the bulk of the fighting force—the North had 4 million, the South just over 1 million. Records of Confederate troop strength were poorly kept or destroyed during the war, but best estimates have placed the total number of enlistments at approximately 1 million. Union enlistments were 2.8 million.

Enlistment rolls alone could be misleading in that soldiers in both armies enlisted for varying amounts of time and sometimes more than once. Nonetheless, this still presents a picture of overwhelming Union superiority in troops it could field. Clement Eaton adds perspective to this disparity in *A History of the Southern Confederacy*. "[The] Confederate Army reached its peak of strength in June 1863 . . . when 261,000 men . . . were reported as present for duty." After this point the Confederate army shrunk in size, "but the Northern Army gained until April 1865 when 622,000 men were present for duty." [9]

By 1862, the South had turned to conscription to alleviate its manpower shortage. However, the benefits of this were significantly lessened by military service exemptions that were granted to planters and overseers on the theory that they were needed to control the slaves. The need for workers with specialized skills also placed a drag on recruitment. Teachers, state workers, railroad employees, druggists, shoemakers, factory and millworkers, blacksmiths, and men from a variety of other occupations were exempted from conscription. As a result, it was mostly unskilled laborers and farmers who were available for military service.

The industrial capacity of the South also compared poorly to that of the North. Shelby Foote noted in *The Civil War,* "The North had 110,000 manufacturing establishments, the South 18,000—1,300,000 industrial workers, compared to 110,000—Massachusetts alone producing over sixty percent more manufactured goods than the whole Confederacy." [10] Until Virginia joined the Confederacy, the South had no foundries capable of making heavy ordnance nor powder mills for making ammunition. By contrast, the Union possessed four large foundries and fifteen armories and arsenals.

The Second American Revolution

In a sense, however, the severe disadvantages Southerners faced strengthened rather than weakened their resolve to fight. To the Confederates, the long odds they faced in confronting the Union on the battlefield was only further proof that they were acting in the spirit of America's founders. Like the patriots who, two generations before, had overcome huge obstacles and defeated the British to achieve independence, Southerners saw their cause as a fight against tyranny—this time against the federal government in Washington. For "the high and solemn motive of defending and protecting the rights . . . which our fathers bequeathed us," Davis called on the South to "renew such sacrifices as our fathers made to the holy cause of constitutional liberty."[11]

Of course, what the Southerners were primarily defending was the right to own slaves. Yet, although slave owners may have stood to benefit most from defense of the Peculiar Institution, the entire Confederacy rallied behind the cause of states' rights. Their rejection of federal power was strong enough to motivate eleven states to secede from the Union and embark on a war whose outcome would affect the entire country. For some, however, the reason for fighting the Union was much simpler. A ragged Virginia soldier captured by Union forces was asked what he was fighting for, if not slavery or states' rights. He replied, "I'm fighting because you're down here."[12]

The Liability of Territorial Advantage

The South, then, saw itself as the wronged party, which provided a boost in morale. Initially the Confederacy enjoyed other advantages as well. First, as defenders of territory the Confederates were in a position to inflict heavy casualties on the North. Second, the Union army would have the burden of defending long supply lines that were subject to attack by Confederate forces. The deeper into the South the Union army went, the more in danger it was of being cut off. Third, the geography of the Confederacy offered natural barriers that impeded movement of Union forces. For example, the Appalachian Mountains, low-lying marshy lands, and major rivers would all have to be over-come in order to assault the Confederate capital of Richmond, Virginia. Unfamiliarity with the terrain and the hostility of the locals to an in-vading army would also play heavily against the North.

These factors did not keep the Union army from invading the South, which it did in force at various points along a one-thousand-mile line that stretched from Virginia to Missouri. Confederate morale, however, was quickly put to the test as Union forces occupied towns and for-aged for supplies. The Confiscation Acts first passed in July 1862 by the Union government authorized the seizure of any property in the South that could be used to make war. These laws were geared to-ward freeing slaves but were widely interpreted to include food, cloth-ing, and any item that could even remotely give aid and comfort to the Confederate military.

Southerners were doubly put upon in that their resources were taken not only by the Union army but also by the Confederate army, which was usually in proximity to its opponent. Both forces would for-age, burn crops to prevent the other side from gaining them, and read-ily seize property from civilians. One Suffolk, Virginia, woman com-plained, "The country will soon be robbed of everything."[13] Eventu-ally, the armies would move on, but the civilians were left behind to eke out an existence with what little remained.

Food and supplies for civilians also became scarce due to an in-adequate transportation system. Major rivers and overland routes came under the increasing control of Union forces. The poor state of the Con-federate railroad system meant that goods could not be moved effi-ciently. For many Southerners, the real tragedy of the situation was that there was enough food, but these transportation problems con-spired to keep it from getting to where it was needed most.

Shortages of food and supplies drove the cost of goods so high that the average person could no longer afford everyday items. Speculation became rampant among unscrupulous Confederate army officers who sold property they had seized to their fellow soldiers and Southern civilians for exorbitant prices.

Civilian miseries in the eastern part of the Confederacy were com-pounded in late 1862 when General Robert E. Lee adopted a scorched-earth policy in hopes of slowing the Union advance through Virginia. He told the secretary of war, "I am loath to add to the devastation which

Making Do with Less

The high cost of carrying on the war in the South brought on shortages of medicine, food, and all manner of everyday items. The Union blockade of Southern ports significantly reduced trade with the outside world, and foraging by Union and Confederate armies alike stripped the land of civilian necessities. Confederates responded to this scarcity in a variety of ways, as E. Merton Coulter notes in *The Confederate States of America, 1861–1865*:

> In the country agricultural leaders advocated more extensive kitchen gardens, and in the cities newspaper editors called for war gardens on any "unoccupied piece of ground large enough to spread a blanket upon." . . . Southerners were advised to raise broomcorn and to produce mustard for medicinal purposes. . . . There were "Confederate needles" from the hawthorn bushes; "Confederate cork" from cypress knees of black-gum roots; "Confederate leather" from cotton cloth for bridle reins and shoe tops . . . rope from Spanish moss, okra stalks, or cotton saturated in tar. . . . The perfect substitute for coffee was sought longest and most assiduously. A famous "Confederate coffee" was made in Richmond of parched peas and corn ground together. Other substitutes eloquently recommended were toasted rye and wheat, chicory, parched garden beets . . . pumpkin seeds and acorns. So absurd were some of the substitutes that now and then a disgusted coffee drinker would remark, "Anything will do, if you don't want coffee."

had already occurred by the ravages of war, and yet think it prudent to throw every impediment to the progress of the enemy toward Richmond in his way." [14]

The Union progress through Virginia could be impeded, as Lee had noted, but it could not be stopped. Furthermore, when Union forces occupied an area, they sought to establish total authority over it with regular patrols and the removal of all Confederate military and civilian leadership. Resistance was dealt with harshly. In response to guerrilla attacks on his forces, Union brigadier general Edward A. Wild exercised the "hard hand of war" on the people of the region. "Finding ordinary measures of little avail, I adopted a more rigorous style of warfare; burned their houses and barns, ate up their livestock, and took hostages from their families." [15]

Being the victims of both Confederate efforts to defend the land and Union efforts to seize it had a corrosive effect on Southern morale.

As Union soldiers advanced into the South in 1862, many Southern families like this one packed their belongings and left their homes behind.

By late 1864, three years of conflict on Southern soil had brought society to the brink of chaos. Roving bands of army deserters pillaged the countryside. Often, exaggerated rumors of Union atrocities forced many to leave their lands as Confederate forces retreated. Many times, those refugees who did return to their homes found them seized by squatters or simply burned to the ground.

State governments appealed to their citizens to police themselves, but this often left towns at the mercy of vigilante bands, some of which committed precisely the crimes—such as theft, robbery, rape, and murder—that they were supposed to prevent. Civilians accused of crimes were brutally punished or executed by Confederate and Union troops alike, which served only to alienate the population and perpetuate lawlessness. A Percy County, Mississippi, tax collector noted, "The civil laws of this state have been trampled under foot by military power which has a very demoralizing effect upon the minds of the citizens." [16]

Recognizing that their government and their army could not protect them left civilians in a desperate state, which was precisely what General William Tecumseh Sherman intended when he marched his army from Atlanta to the sea at the end of 1864. He said of his objective, "If we can march a well-appointed army right through [President Davis's] territory, it is a demonstration to the world, foreign and domestic, that we have a power which Davis cannot resist." [17]

A Rich Man's War, but a Poor Man's Fight

The harsh consequences the war visited on the South exaggerated the disparity that existed between the rich and the poor, worsening the decline in morale. For their part, slave owners saw defense of slavery as a defense of a way of life. "The institution of slavery had engendered in the master class a fierce and quixotic pride," Eaton notes. "The evolution of their society had nourished a romantic spirit which placed honor and prestige high among human values." [18] Such concepts, however, were lost on the poor of the South, who were already barely able to feed themselves. Families and entire communities slipped into poverty so profound that they could no longer justify their sacrifice to the cause.

The impact of the war on the majority of Southerners contrasted sharply with its consequences for the nation's leaders. The men who ran the Confederacy operated with the interests of the planter class at heart. The Sequestration Act passed in June 1861 was but one example of this. This act called for the seizure of the property and personal effects of Northerners who owned estates in the South. However, the proceeds from the sale of such seizures went not for the purposes of fighting the war, but instead went into a separate fund that reimbursed those who lost property to similar Union confiscations, and the beneficiaries were usually members of the planter class.

The most grievous example of the special treatment rich planters enjoyed was the Twenty Slave Law. This act granted exemption from military service to planters who owned twenty or more slaves. Poor farmers who could never hope to afford to own slaves saw this as blatant favoritism of the planter aristocracy. Combined with the fact that many plantation owners were still planting cotton despite tremendous food shortages, this exemption was taken by the lower classes as a sign that the rich did not have the will to fight or sacrifice for the war that they had called for in the first place.

Recognizing that they were fighting a losing battle to defend an institution that they knew they would not benefit from, many Confederate soldiers deserted from their units. William Dickey, a company commander in the Georgia militia, wrote, "There is some demoralization in this army no doubt, and more of it than I like to hear of." [19]

Further desertions from Confederate service resulted from the poor quality of matériel and the lack of food and clothing. By the end of 1864, when victory seemed most remote, soldiers thought it better to return to their suffering families than fight for a hopeless cause. Deserters found sympathy among civilians who fed, hid, and otherwise supported them. "So common is the crime [of desertion], it has in popular estimation lost the stigma which justly pertains to it," [20] remarked Assistant Secretary of War John Campbell. By war's end, Confederate commanders had recorded over one hundred thousand desertions from the army.

An Empty Sacrifice

The deteriorating morale resulted not just from a sense of the inevitability of military defeat but also from the realization that Southerners were sacrificing both the institution of slavery and the cause of states' rights in search of victory. Doubts over the wisdom of slavery had increased throughout the war, partly motivated by the high cost of maintaining and policing slaves in a nation suffering from food and manpower shortages. The most radical idea, however, was that of enlisting slaves as soldiers in the Confederate army. The concept was widely rejected, with one critic calling it "monstrous" and "revolting to Southern sentiment, Southern pride, and Southern honor." [21]

Jefferson Davis thought differently, especially after casualties, disease, and desertion had thoroughly depleted the ranks of the Southern armies. A bill narrowly passed the Confederate Congress on March 13, 1865, that would compensate owners for slaves who were sent to fight and calling for the slaves themselves to be freed upon the completion of their service, provided they served well. This act came too late to be of any use, as Lee surrendered to Union general Ulysses S. Grant barely three weeks later, but it was symbolic of the debate over just how far Southerners would go in order to win the war.

How freeing slaves would preserve slavery eluded most Southerners. They were angered that their own government would consider extending its power over the master-slave relationship, an area into which it had never dared tread before. This action was but one of many intrusions on states' rights that included conscription, impressment, and the nationalization of state resources that troubled Confederates throughout the war. Irrespective of the fact that Davis's actions were in the interest of saving the nation, Southerners felt they were merely

---

 ## The Free State of Jones

Throughout the South, loyalists to the Union aided Union troops and actively fought against the Confederate army. One such enclave was the rural farming community of Jones County, Mississippi, in 1861, where there were few slaves and great distrust of the Confederate government. When secession came to a vote, they went against the majority of the state and chose to remain in the Union by a count of 376 to 24.

Loyalist leader Newton Knight recalled years later what happened next, in this excerpt from Victoria E. Bynum's *The Free State of Jones: Mississippi's Longest Civil War:*

> "The next thing we knew," said Newt, "they were conscripting us. The rebels passed a law conscripting everybody between 18 and 35. They just come around with a squad of soldiers [and] took you." But, he maintained, "if they had a right to conscript me when I didn't want to fight the Union, I had a right to quit when I got ready."

Fearing for the safety of their families, Knight and many others deserted and returned home. The men and women of Jones County established a pro-Union government, drove out pro-Confederate authorities, and resolved to pay no local, state, or Confederate tax. In October 1864, county elections were held under the watchful eye of the Confederate army, and pro-Confederate candidates rose to office. However, Knight and his followers would remain loyal to the Union throughout the war.

exchanging one centralized government for another. Distrustful of centralized government as they were, many Southerners could not believe that those powers would ever be rescinded, even if the Confederacy achieved independence.

The assumption by the Confederate government of powers that properly belonged to the states, along with actions that would free slaves in the South, negated the sacrifices that were being made for the Southern cause. Deprived of their original cause for fighting, Southerners no longer had the will to continue the struggle. However, a central government that was deliberately created without the power it needed to fight a war was left with few choices in the pursuit of victory.

Confederate Politics: Fighting the Union and Each Other

Chapter 2

If a monument is ever erected as a symbolical gravestone over the "lost cause," it should have engraved upon it these words: "Died of State Rights."

Frank L. Owsley, *State Rights in the Confederacy*

THE PRINCIPAL MOTIVATION for creating the Confederate States of America was to address what Southerners viewed as the usurping of their rights by the federal government. With this in mind, the central government of the Confederacy was deliberately crafted so that the rights of the states would never be overridden by a federal entity. Many Southern leaders, including several state governors, believed that the preservation of states' rights—even more than slavery—was the single most important responsibility of the new nation, and they zealously defended those rights against any encroachment, no matter the consequence of doing so.

This passionate self-interest on the part of the states severely hampered the South's prosecution of the war and led to intense conflict between Jefferson Davis and many state governors. States' rights proponents often responded to Davis's assumption of broad powers to defend the nation with derision and outright defiance. Virtually every decision made in regard to the conduct of the war—from raising and leading an army to the very strategy with which the Confederacy should defend itself from the Union—was opposed in some fashion by the states.

Recognizing the corrosive effect this struggle was having on the Confederate cause, South Carolina governor Francis Pickens, in an

April 1862 letter to his colleagues, noted, "Unless the States bring forward their power and resources to sustain the common government, and put forth all their local energies to defend our organization, we will feel the fatal consequences." [22] State leaders, however, often could not see past their own independence, even when the way of life they cherished was threatened with annihilation.

Impaired by Their Own Constitution

The independence of the individual states was enshrined in the Confederacy's Constitution, which was completed on March 11, 1861, and subsequently ratified by the first Southern states to secede from the Union. The document was closely modeled after the Constitution of the United States, with certain exceptions. Most notable among these was that slavery was explicitly protected in the Confederate document, and the right of property in the form of slaves was guaranteed in all Southern states.

The imposition of state sovereignty was also clearly defined in the Confederate document by two significant changes. The preamble—"We, the People of the Confederate States, each State acting in its sovereign and independent character," [23]—essentially defined the Confederacy as a whole that was less than the sum of its parts. Also, the phrase calling for the government to "promote the general welfare" of the citizenry, found in the U.S. document, was removed. This mandate had allowed the federal government to act in what it deemed the nation's best interest. Southerners felt that the central government should have no such right to decide what constituted the general welfare and that the pursuit of collective interests of the states could not justify denying the particular interests of a single state.

Deleting the general welfare clause, however, created a serious impediment to the Confederate government's ability to conduct the war. States could not be compelled to come to the material aid of other states in need, nor could the Confederate Congress compel the states to act for the benefit of the nation as a whole. Davis continuously pushed the constitutional boundaries created by these provisions in order to defend the Confederacy against the Union, but he consistently met with opposition from men who, like Alabama delegate Robert H. Smith, believed that "however wise and beneficent may be the working of the

Alexander Stephens and Robert Toombs: Confederate Founding Fathers

Secessionist leaders gathered in Montgomery, Alabama, on February 4, 1861, to set a course of action for their new nation. Many different plans were introduced by the several state delegations, but none was so bold as the "Georgia project," a strategy set forth by Alexander Stephens and Robert Toombs. William C. Davis explains their vision in *The Union That Shaped the Confederacy: Robert Toombs and Alexander Stephens:*

> The boldness of the plan was breathtaking. The delegates had no elective or appointive power to do this. They would be acting entirely on their own initiative, and at the risk that their states . . . might repudiate what they did. They would raise taxes, start an army and a navy, frame provisional and permanent constitutions, and establish foreign relations, all without a jot of lawful authority. They would choose and install in power a president for whom not one Southern citizen other than themselves would have had an opportunity to vote. In seeking to redress the shortcomings of democracy they had suffered in the Union, they would establish and operate for a brief period the most undemocratically conceived ruling body ever seen on the continent.

Some of their colleagues viewed such actions as hasty, but Stephens and Toombs recognized the severity of the situation facing the South. However, they would not hold this pragmatic view when Davis later proposed equally bold measures to fight the war.

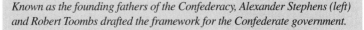
Known as the founding fathers of the Confederacy, Alexander Stephens (left) and Robert Toombs drafted the framework for the Confederate government.

General Government, it is to State action we must mainly look for the advancement which shall secure high civilization." [24]

A Divisive Leadership

The tendency of the individual states' leaders to pursue their respective interests was intensified by the personality of Jefferson Davis himself. When Davis was chosen to lead the Confederacy, he was considered the most capable man for the job. He was unanimously elected president by the state delegations at the Montgomery, Alabama, Constitutional Convention in February 1861, but that unanimity was superficial. Each state had voted as a bloc, masking the divisions over Davis's selection that existed within each delegation. Opposition to his leadership became apparent almost immediately. Within days of Davis's assuming office, Congressman Thomas R.R. Cobb of Georgia remarked, "Many are already regretting his election." [25]

The Confederate president's personality contributed to his problems. Davis possessed an autocratic nature that showed itself particularly in dealings with his cabinet. Never one to worry about the feelings or sensibilities of others, he tended to alienate many of the people he worked with. Robert Kean, head of the Bureau of War, noted that Davis "seems to possess a most unenviable facility for converting friends into enemies." [26] As a consequence, otherwise capable cabinet secretaries resigned, citing an inability to work with Davis. The result was a lack of steady leadership in the various government departments. Over the course of the war, the six cabinet offices changed hands fourteen times.

Another cause for discord within Davis's administration was his capacity for getting caught up in administrative minutiae. He absorbed virtually every correspondence that crossed his desk and often took on mundane administrative duties better left to subordinates. Secretary of War George W. Randolph remarked that he "does not discriminate between important and unimportant matters." [27] He held cabinet meetings into the late night hours until men were haggard with exhaustion. Davis also imposed his own views on the various departments, habitually rejecting the advice the cabinet secretaries had been appointed to provide. Davis's domineering hand motivated one critic to view the true makeup of the cabinet as "Secretary of State,

Honorable Jeff. Davis of Mississippi; War and Navy, Jeff. Davis of Mississippi; Interior, ex-Senator Davis of Mississippi; Treasury, Col. Davis of Mississippi; Attorney General, Mr. Davis of Mississippi."[28]

Thanks to his domination of the government, Davis became a focal point for criticism with every setback the Confederacy suffered during the war. Many of the attacks against him were, however, motivated as much by personal animosity as by professional disagreement. Davis's critics never formed an organized opposition to his leadership, but their attacks did tend to erode public confidence in his administration. In the end, his keen intellect and administrative experience, which could have greatly benefited the Confederate cause,

Confederate president Jefferson Davis (seated center, left) meets with Southern leaders in 1863. Davis's autocratic governing style created tension within his administration.

were dissipated by his micromanagement of the presidency and his insufferable personality.

Losing the Support of the Vice President

The single most detrimental blow that Davis's abrasive personality delivered the government was in alienating Vice President Alexander Stephens. The Confederate vice president enjoyed near unanimous support at the outset of his term, and he counted among his allies such powerful Georgia politicians as Robert Toombs and Governor Joseph E. Brown. Even though Davis and Stephens were "at odds on every important political measure since 1845,"[29] in the early days of the Confederacy Stephens dutifully defended the president from the attacks of his enemies. Davis, on the other hand, did not come to the similar aid of his vice president, who also suffered the scathing criticism of political opponents who saw him as vain and egotistical.

The president routinely neglected to keep Stephens informed, which further damaged their relationship. Since Davis rarely consulted with Stephens over cabinet appointments and policy decisions, the vice president, in his quest for information, had to poke around telegraph offices and scan newspapers like a common citizen, a circumstance he found insulting for a man in his position. Eventually, Stephens developed an acute lack of interest in the office, which, combined with his chronic poor health, motivated him to return to his home state of Georgia, where he spent most of his time after 1863.

The president and vice president also had significant differences over policy. For instance, Stephens had little tolerance for Davis's calls for the suspension of the writ of habeas corpus, which gave the president power to jail disloyal citizens and hold them indefinitely without trial. Congress passed acts suspending the writ of habeas corpus in 1862, 1863, and 1864; all were restricted in scope to areas threatened with Union invasion and were designed to expire after a specified period of time. For his part, Stephens was an unyielding proponent of state sovereignty, personal liberty, and the Confederate Constitution as he understood it. So, by February 15, 1864, when Congress, at the president's request, passed a third act suspending habeas corpus, Stephens had made the transition from Davis's impotent vice president to his vocal public opponent. In an address to the Georgia legislature on March 16, Stephens called the suspension of the writ "unwise, impolitic, unconstitutional." [30] He also told his brother Linton, a Georgia legislator, "Since [Davis's] inauguration, his every act is consistent with the course of a weak timid shy unprincipled arch aspirant after absolute power by usurpation." [31]

In publicly opposing his president and shirking the responsibilities of his office, Stephens played a role in the breakdown of his relationship with Davis. However, as Thomas E. Schott notes in *Alexander H. Stephens of Georgia: A Biography,* in losing Stephens's support, Davis "blundered seriously in casting aside the man himself. The vice president was a political force to be reckoned with." [32]

"She Died of States' Rights"

The emergence of Stephens as an opponent to Davis's policies emboldened the states' rights faction in the Confederacy and further complicated attempts to prosecute the war. Almost from the beginning, Davis found himself in conflict with several state governors over his exercising of broad wartime powers. Responding to criticism of the war effort, Secretary of War Judah Benjamin noted on November 4, 1861, "The difficulty lies with the Governors of the States who are unwilling to trust the common defense to one common head. . . . Each Governor wants to satisfy his own people. . . . The voice of reason is stilled." [33]

One of the first controversial steps taken to aid the war effort was the institution of an impressment policy. This act authorized the War Department to seize property of any description that could be considered a military necessity, including crops, building materials, and slaves. The policy was widely opposed by the states, which sought redress in the courts. Suing the states for the right to impress sorely needed supplies on a case-by-case basis would have taken more time than the Confederate government was willing to allow. The Justice Department replied, "The Government will not, under any circumstances, enter the State Courts and go through a process of litigation whenever it is necessary to obtain supplies of any kind for the army." [34] Since legal action proved useless in their fight against impressment, the state governors took matters into their own hands.

North Carolina governor Zebulon Vance threatened to burn his state's blockade-runners after Davis ordered that half of the ships' cargo space be allocated for military purposes.

North Carolina governor Zebulon Vance responded to the allocation of up to one-half of the cargo space in blockade-runners for military purposes by threatening to burn the ships. Alabama governor Andrew B. Moore refused to allow the state's agents to collect Confederate taxes. When the Confederate army sought to remove rails from the Florida railroad for use in more strategically disadvantaged areas, Governor John Milton filed an injunction and threatened the army officers with arrest. Yet, no act by the central government met with more widespread government derision than the Conscription Act.

In his February 18, 1861, inaugural address, Davis called on the Confederate Congress to create an army. States' rights advocates expressed discomfort with the prospect of an army controlled by the central government, and naturally preferred their own respective state militias. "Under ordinary circumstances" Davis recognized that the Confederacy "could rely mainly upon the militia." However, "in the present condition of affairs . . . there should be a well-instructed and disciplined army."[35] Congress acted on Davis's request, but the one hundred thousand volunteers that came forward soon proved too few. Gen-

---

 ## The Confederate Press Has Its Say

Newspapers offered editors and politicians an excellent opportunity to disseminate their views across the South. Some papers, like Robert Barnwell Rhett's *Charleston Mercury* and the *Richmond Examiner,* edited by Edward A. Pollard, expressed almost constant opposition to Jefferson Davis and his policies. George C. Rable explains the impact of the Southern press in *The Confederate Republic: A Revolution Against Politics:*

> Although hardly exempt from provincialism and selfishness, the Southern press generally sustained the president and worked to build a national consciousness. Newspapers were a prime source of political information in a predominantly rural society and shaped a political culture still dependent on the oral transmission of news and opinions.

> Yet editorial opposition exerted influence through the sheer stridency of its rhetoric. Vilifying the "pimps and parasites" who supported the Richmond government and denouncing the "venal self-seekers or base panderers to executive power," Robert Barnwell Rhett sought to make the president's reputation "subservient to . . . the redemption and salvation of the Confederate States." Or in other words, make Jefferson Davis subservient to Robert Barnwell Rhett.

> Rhett sarcastically suggested that Davis stop trying to be a Washington, a Jackson, or a Calhoun . . . the president could select a better cabinet (i.e. Rhett or his followers) and leave military strategy to the generals, or at least to generals approved by [South Carolina] radicals.

erals Robert E. Lee and Joseph E. Johnston called for conscription, and on March 28, 1862, Davis recommended the idea to Congress.

The Conscription Act, passed by the Confederate Congress on April 16, 1862, was the first such law ever enacted on the American continent. It required all able-bodied men between eighteen and thirty-five years of age to join the Confederate army for a period of three years or until the war ended. On September 27, 1862, the act was amended to include all men up to forty-five years of age; on February 17, 1864, it was amended again to include all men ages seventeen to fifty. In addition to slave owners who qualified under the Twenty Slave Law, exemptions were also granted to those who were physically incapable of serving and to men whose professions were otherwise necessary to the war effort, such as railroad employees, blacksmiths, and factory workers.

Governor Joseph E. Brown of Georgia vocally opposed conscription, calling it "subversion of [Georgia's] sovereignty, and at war with all the principles for the support of which Georgia entered into this revolution." [36] The Georgia state courts, along with courts in other states, upheld the constitutionality of the law, but Brown did everything he could to hamper its implementation, vowing, "The people of Georgia will refuse to yield their sovereignty to usurpation." [37] He insisted that Georgia troops be commanded by Georgia officers in the field and would not allow them to leave the state carrying state-owned weapons. Brown and North Carolina's governor Vance pushed their respective states' delegations in Congress to greatly expand the list of exemptions from service that could be granted. By war's end, Brown issued more than fifteen thousand exemptions from military service, in many cases as favors to state officials and political supporters.

Throughout the war, Brown was Davis's staunchest opponent, and his consternation with the Confederate government did not end with the debate over conscription. Like Vance of North Carolina, Brown was a fierce guardian of states' rights, and he was keenly jealous of his own power as governor. He took the assertion of Georgia's sovereignty quite literally, going as far as sending an emissary to England to seek separate recognition of his state from Queen Victoria. He delayed allowing the transfer of former federal arms to the Confederacy and

A contemporary political cartoon shows a Southerner being pressed into military service. The Conscription Act of 1862 required all able-bodied men to enlist in the Confederate army.

often kept the best weapons and matériel for his own state's armory. Whenever Davis issued one of his several proclamations calling for days of fasting and prayer in support of the troops, Brown would reject the order, issuing his own identical state proclamations a week later.

Brown's battle with Davis extended to the debate over the suspension of habeas corpus, and he joined Vice President Stephens in this particular fight. There were many opponents to the habeas corpus measures throughout the South, but Davis saw no other way to combat the disloyal elements that were aiding the enemy in this time of crisis. After Georgia was invaded in 1864, Brown openly considered the war a failure, noting that the government in Richmond had abandoned the principles of "all self-government and the sovereignty of the States."[38]

To the detriment of the South, men like Brown, Vance, and Stephens interpreted their enemy to be Davis and his administration in Richmond, and they focused their energies on the fight with the Confederate government rather than with the Union army that had invaded and occupied their land. Sovereignty was their paramount concern. As E. Merton Coulter notes in *The Confederate States of America, 1861–1865*, "They were fighting for their rights, forgetting their independence must come before those rights could be permanently established."[39]

A Muddled Military Strategy

Political opposition went beyond broad philosophical concerns, to the point of forcing Davis to accommodate the sovereignty of the Southern states in formulating military strategy. The states' concern with their individual defense rather than the defense of the Confederacy as a whole obligated Davis to support spreading the army along the northern border and allowing several states a role in the military plan. Davis was willing to grant states a major role in their own defense, believing that the very size of the Confederacy would prevent its downfall. "There are no vital points on the preservation of which the continued existence of the Confederacy depends," Davis noted. "There is no military success of the enemy which can accomplish its destruction."[40]

 ## Pursuing a Separate Peace

By 1864 many Southerners had grown tired of war. Movements for separate peace agreements with the Union gained strength in North Carolina and Georgia. The extent of the movement in North Carolina, where leading peace activist William W. Holden challenged Governor Vance's reelection, is illustrated in George C. Rable's *The Confederate Republic: A Revolution Against Politics:*

> Beginning in late July, nearly one hundred meetings were held in at least thirty counties. Peace petitions—reportedly printed in Holden's office—denounced Confederate violations of civil liberties and called for a new convention to protect the people's rights and interests either by opening negotiations with the Northern states or by withdrawing North Carolina from the Confederacy.

In Georgia Union General William T. Sherman reached out to Alexander Stephens and Governor Brown, playing on their discontent with Davis and offering a painless occupation of the state if it withdrew from the Confederacy. Robert Toombs advised Stephens, as quoted in William C. Davis's *The Union That Shaped the Confederacy: Robert Toombs and Alexander Stephens,* "Do not by any means go to see Sherman. It will place you in a wrong, very wrong position."

Stephens heeded Toombs's advice, Brown did not accept Sherman's offer, and in North Carolina, Vance defeated Holden. The peace movement, which gave voice to a war-weary faction, had failed.

Robert E. Lee, appointed General in Chief of the Armies on March 13, 1862, disagreed with Davis's defensive strategy, proposing instead a massive concentration of troops in one area, with the desired effect of delivering a blow so crippling and decisive to the Union that Northern support for the war would crumble. Robert Toombs echoed this sentiment when he suggested a direct attack on Washington, D.C. Davis, however, realizing that individual states would not agree to such a concentration of their troops in one place, decided against this strategy.

As it turned out both Davis and Lee were wrong. Lee, in believing that "the enemy cannot attack all points at one time,"[41] was gravely mistaken. The Union did have the resources to adapt a wide-scale offensive strategy, and by the end of the first year of fighting had opened up fronts in Virginia, Louisiana, Kentucky, Tennessee, and Mississippi. On the other hand, the thin line of defense that Davis had proposed did not hold against the multipronged Union onslaught. Davis then compounded his miscalculation by continuing to support the original defensive plan, believing that the farther the Union army moved from its base of supply, the more vulnerable it would be to attack. What Davis did not realize was that the Union's offensive strategy took into account the logistical needs of its invading armies. By capturing Southern supplies, the Union was able to meet the basic requirements of its forces and deplete vital resources the Confederates relied on to defend themselves. This simultaneously weakened the Southern defense and accelerated Union occupation of Confederate territory.

While Davis was constrained by a need to oblige the states in his war plans, his obstinate maintenance of a defensive strategy was also a reflection on his autocratic nature. Lee was moved to the command of the Army of Northern Virginia on June 1, 1862, and the position of general in chief remained unfilled for eighteen months, with Davis preferring to rely on his own military knowledge to guide the Confederate forces. Eventually he gave the post to the unremarkable General Braxton Bragg during 1864 but continued to depend on his own judgment. By the time Lee was reassigned to the position on January 26, 1865, the setbacks the Confederate forces had suffered were nearly irreversible.

Within his cabinet, Davis's military adjutant and inspector general Samuel Cooper offered little advice or strategic vision, serving instead as a glorified administrative clerk. The five different men who would serve as secretary of war during the four years of fighting all clashed with Davis over strategic issues, and the high rate of turnover in that cabinet office perpetuated the confused military situation. This chaotic, combative, and unproductive atmosphere would ultimately extend to the commanders in the field who, in turn, endured their own institutional conflicts brought on by pride and fierce individualism.

Flawed Military Leadership

Chapter 3

The wise general used the spirit of the army with prudence and discretion, and his army responded with triumph against incredible obstacles and with steadfastness in crisis. Less wise generals squandered it trying to compensate for failures in planning or in logistics, or in battlefield coordination, and their armies suffered tragedy either with Pyrrhic victories or devastating defeats.

Thomas B. Buell, *The Warrior Generals:*
Combat Leadership in the Civil War

AS MUCH AS any other factor, the inability of Confederate battlefield commanders to work in a cohesive and objective manner brought about Southern defeat in the Civil War. In a society that placed a high value on honor, these men vainly guarded their reputations and readily challenged anyone they felt had attacked their dignity. Vanity also led each of the generals to believe his own command to be the key army in Confederate defense; as a result, struggles erupted over the distribution of strategic and logistical support. These bitter rivalries led to insubordination and damaged morale, ultimately interfering with the war effort.

Political meddling in military affairs likewise created leadership problems for the armies. In order to placate state governors, President Davis appointed numerous men to command positions who had little or no military experience. Their costly blunders and unremitting egotism drew disdain from seasoned generals whose jobs were made tougher as a result. Politicians also used pressure to influence strategic decisions in favor of their respective states, often disregarding the broader military situation, which steadily deteriorated in large part due to this narrow-minded self-interest.

The Departmental System

In order for the Confederate war effort to be successful, cohesion needed to exist between the various armies working to defeat the Union forces. Commanders also required an administrative framework in which to make the intricate decisions necessary in battle in a timely fashion. A system of regional military departments was created to address these issues, with each departmental commander given independent authority over the offensive and defensive operations in his jurisdiction, leaving only the most vital strategic decisions to Davis in Richmond.

This system suffered from several flaws, among them the diversion of considerable manpower to run the various subcommands. Thomas L. Connelly and Archer Jones note in *The Politics of Command: Factions and Ideas in the Confederate Strategy* that "every department, however unimportant, usually possessed an extensive staff connected with departmental headquarters, a second body of officers serving in district or subdistrict commands, and a third series of outpost commands."[42]

The government in Richmond added to this bureaucratic tangle with its frequent reorganization of the departmental jurisdictions and the continuous reassignment of commanders and field personnel. The government also sent mixed signals in the inconsistency of delegating authority to these commanders. For instance, Davis granted so much local authority for the 1862 invasion of Kentucky that neither General Braxton Bragg nor Edmund Kirby Smith was clear who was in charge or what their objective was. After the invasion began, however, the government detached portions of Bragg's department without his knowledge, effectively leaving him without the troops and supplies he needed to ensure success. As a consequence, the Confederate invasion of Kentucky was turned back by Union forces.

Disagreement also existed among the generals as to which region was the most important or most in need of support. Connelly and Jones point out that, among the generals, there was a "myopic [near-sighted] concern for one's own army and region [that] was certainly endemic to the Confederate high command."[43] Examples of this include General P.G.T. Beauregard, who put forward several strategic proposals calling for a massive troop concentration in the west; yet, in 1863 he reversed position, protesting against shifting troops from his South Carolina department west to Mississippi. General Joseph E. Johnston likewise protested having to reinforce Chattanooga, Tennessee, in the late summer of 1863, despite having actively urged moving troops to the Tennessee front the previous year.

Robert E. Lee also exhibited self-interest in his command decisions and proposals. Davis had continued to seek Lee's advice after he reassigned the general to command the Army of Northern Virginia, and Lee often proposed strategies that revolved around what the other Confederate armies could do to help him. In June 1862, for example, he suggested moving the Georgia and Carolina forces to open a second front in Virginia. In September, he proposed moving the Army of Tennessee to hold Richmond while he invaded Maryland. And, after his defeat at Gettysburg, Lee advised Davis that Beauregard's

Confederate generals such as (from left) Braxton Bragg, Joseph Johnston, and P.G.T. Beauregard were in constant disagreement over military strategy.

South Carolina forces should be transferred to Virginia. "Richmond must not be given up!"[44] Lee vowed with tears in his eyes.

The Fractured High Command

Lee's provincial belief that Virginia alone was the key to the continued existence of the Confederacy hampered his abilities to provide a cohesive plan that Davis could work with. Yet, when it came to dealing with the personalities of his generals, Lee would be the least of Davis's concerns.

Problems in the Confederate high command started almost immediately after the onset of the war. On May 16, 1861, the general staff was created with Adjutant Samuel Cooper in the top position. Following him in rank order were Albert Sidney Johnston, Robert E. Lee, Joseph E. Johnston, and P.G.T. Beauregard. Joseph Johnston resented his placement in this chain of command, believ-

Lee's Unanswered Call to Maryland

In response to calls from Confederate sympathizers looking to secede from the Union, Lee took his army into Maryland on September 8, 1862. He hoped to capitalize on the sentiments of the population in a bid to defeat Union forces and draw the state into the Confederacy. Lee issued a proclamation to the people of Maryland explaining his intentions, excerpted here from Thomas B. Buell's *The Warrior Generals: Combat Leadership in the Civil War:*

> Under the pretense of supporting the Constitution, but in violation of its most valuable provisions, your citizens have been arrested and imprisoned upon no charge . . . the government of your chief City has been usurped by armed strangers; your Legislature has been dissolved by the unlawful arrest of its members, freedom of the press and of speech has been suppressed. . . .
>
> Believing that the People of Maryland possessed a spirit too lofty to submit to such a government, the people of the South have long wished to aid you in throwing off this foreign yoke. . . .
>
> In obedience to this wish, our Army has come among you, and is prepared to assist you with the power of its arms in regaining the rights of which you have been despoiled.

Lee's call to the people of Maryland went unheeded, and when his forces entered the state, they were confronted by a largely disinterested populace that had no desire to join the Confederacy.

ing that his military rank prior to the war entitled him to the top spot. He told Davis that his present assignment was "in violation of my rights as an officer, of the plighted faith of the Confederacy, and of the Constitution and laws of the land."[45] Davis refused to concede to Johnston's demand for higher status, and the issue remained a source of animosity between the two men for the duration of the war.

Beauregard also ran afoul of Davis after the July 21, 1861, Battle of Manassas, known in the North as the Battle of Bull Run. When Beauregard failed to pursue the Union forces in their panicked retreat from the field, he was accused by politicians and the press of passing up a valuable opportunity to crush the federal army and bring the war to a swift conclusion. In reality, the Confederate army was not much better organized than the Union's, and Beauregard had resisted pursuit because of want of supplies and lack of coordination. Nevertheless, controversy erupted when Beauregard's report on the battle was interpreted in the press as an indictment of Davis's plan of attack. Pride on the part of both men played a role in escalating their disagreement over proper military procedure and resulted in Beauregard's transfer to the West.

Fighting among the generals was also rampant. General Thomas "Stonewall" Jackson arrested Ambrose P. Hill twice for insubordination—once for telling Jackson, "You're not fit to be a general."[46] Hill's mouth also got him in trouble with General James Longstreet. Bragg's command of the Army of Tennessee in 1863 was under continuous strain from his lieutenants Leonidas Polk and William J. Hardee, who openly disobeyed his orders and exhibited a complete lack of respect for his authority. Meanwhile, Major General John C. Pemberton's troops threatened mutiny if left under his command.

Robert Toombs, a political appointee with inadequate military skills, fought with everybody. So difficult was Toombs's personality that one critic noted, "Bob Toombs disagrees with himself between meals."[47] He exhibited a disdain for generals from West Point and considered them a group of elitists. He believed Lee's appointment to commander of the Army of Northern Virginia was an example of cronyism and once challenged Major General D.H. Hill to a duel over accusations relating to Toombs's poor command in the Battle of Malvern Hill.

Infighting among Confederate generals was extremely common. Robert Toombs, a general with a notoriously difficult personality, frequently squabbled with his cohorts.

He was disgusted by Joseph Johnston's idleness in the West and said that Johnston "was only put in command to annoy gentlemen. I never knew as incompetent an executive officer." [48]

Politics Gets in the Way

In fact, it was Toombs who lacked competence, but he was not the only one. Two hundred twenty-six Confederate generals were rank military amateurs and had no formal training as officers nor any education in military tactics. Among these men were a group referred to as political generals for having earned their appointments through patronage rather than military skill. Their pursuit of glory led them into the Confederate army because, as Thomas B. Buell notes, "for Southerners, glory was on the battlefield."[49] There was more glamour and respectability to found in combat than in politics. Those who were motivated to command a regiment or a brigade for this reason alone generally had little to contribute to the war effort.

Davis, however, could not reject these political generals because the 187 professionally trained generals that he had at his disposal were not numerous enough to run the entire Confederate army. Political concerns also had to be taken into account. Some of the politicians who sought military service had the power to injure the president for not gratifying their ambitions. Governor Zebulon Vance believed his state was being discriminated against in military appointments, noting, "It is mortifying to find entire brigades of North Carolina soldiers in the field commanded by strangers."[50] To avoid a politically damaging fight, Davis placated him by reassigning North Carolina commanders to the state's regiments.

Many Southerners, particularly politicians, believed that the political generals would be a benefit to the war effort. Indeed, at first their sacrifice to the cause boosted morale and worked as an inducement for their constituents to enlist. The errors these political generals made on the battlefield, however, and the resultant losses in men, matériel, and morale, often negated any benefits provided by their initial appointments.

On occasion, a general's incompetence was so extreme that it served the Union better than the Confederacy. Brigadier General Gideon Pillow was one such appointee. His poor command at Fort Donelson failed to break the Union lines and led to a siege and loss of the garrison. He managed to avoid capture by slipping away, leaving a subordinate to surrender to General Grant. When told by one of the Confederates of Pillow's escape, Grant was unconcerned, noting, "I would rather have him in command of you fellows than a prisoner."[51]

Politicians also sought influence over strategy, gathering with family members and supporters of various generals into factions called blocs. One such faction, the Western Concentration bloc, was actually a collection of smaller blocs united in their concern for the central South. The Abingdon-Columbia bloc sought the advancement of Joseph Johnston's military career. The Kentucky bloc consisted of Kentuckians hoping for a Confederate conquest of their state. The anti-Bragg bloc sought Bragg's removal from command in Tennessee and lobbied for his replacement by either Johnston or Beauregard.

Interference by the Western Concentration bloc and other politicians in the war effort proved costly. Motivated by self-interest and proceeding with less than full knowledge of the military situation, they made deadly mistakes on the field that further eroded the Confederacy's already slim chance of defeating the Union. Conversely, it was one general's inability to read a political situation that would prove to be one of the gravest mistakes the Confederate army would make during the war.

Costly Battlefield Mistakes

Incompetence could also take the form of misreading the political landscape, and in one case the mistake was catastrophic. On May 16, 1861, the Kentucky legislature voted 69-26 to remain neutral in the War Between the States, hoping to avoid sacrificing their unique political position. Kentucky had more slaveholders than any other Southern state outside of Georgia and Virginia, but it also enjoyed a greater trade relationship with the North. Lincoln likened the state's neutrality to a rejection of the Union, and therefore illegal, but he was willing to bide his time, fearing that any intervention might push the state into the Confederacy. Lincoln illustrated the importance of the state in his grand strategy when he said, "I hope to have God on my side, but I must have Kentucky."[52]

Davis similarly recognized the unique situation that Kentucky posed, realizing that, while the state had not sided with the Confederacy, it was not part of the Union either and was, therefore, an ally. Kentucky also provided a natural barrier between the South and the North, which therefore protected Tennessee from attack. However, the advantage that Kentucky's neutrality afforded the Confederacy disappeared on September 4, 1861.

General Leonidas Polk moved his forces into the western Kentucky city of Paducah, a city so open in its Southern sentiment that it

In September 1861, General Leonidas Polk marched into Paducah, Kentucky, hoping the presence of his troops would sway the state's population to the Confederate cause.

was nicknamed "Little Charleston." Polk hoped to capitalize on the pro-Southern attitudes in the state, believing that the appearance of Confederate troops would swing Kentucky toward the South. Polk's supposition was wrong. The fiercely neutral Kentuckians were angry at this armed display and remained hostile to the Confederate presence. Grant entered the state from the North, proclaiming his intention to protect Kentucky from the rebel invaders. Polk was pushed out and Kentucky sided with the North, opening a path for Union forces to charge into Tennessee and from there into the Deep South.

Missing the Larger Picture

Sometimes the problem was not so much incompetence as it was missing the larger strategic picture. Such was the situation with Lee, whose continued desire to assume the offensive put his forces in serious danger. In May 1863, he proposed to Davis an invasion of the North. His plan called for a march into Pennsylvania to the Susquehanna River, where he would cut the railroad lines and disrupt the coal supply to New York City and the ships anchored there. The broader goal of this offensive would be to take the pressure off Virginia by forcing the Union Army of the Potomac to engage Lee deep in federal territory, where he intended to destroy it. Such a victory would bring panic to Washington, strike a political blow in the North against Lincoln's war effort, and hopefully gain the long-sought support of nations in Europe.

Davis had reason to be skeptical of the wisdom of such a bold move. During this time the Confederate garrison at Vicksburg, Mississippi, was under siege by Grant's forces. General John C. Pemberton, the garrison's commander, desperately needed reinforcements to prevent collapse and the loss of control of the Mississippi River to the Union. The Army of Northern Virginia was an obvious source of reinforcements, but Lee refused to allow a division to be drawn from his command, remarking, "The uncertainty of its arrival and the uncertainty of its application cause me to doubt the policy of sending it."[53] Lee insisted that his own invasion into Pennsylvania would offset any loss suffered at Vicksburg and deliver a significant boost to Southern morale that would fuel future battlefield successes.

Lee's invasion of the North was ill-advised. The death of General Jackson, whom Lee referred to as his right arm, just weeks before had created a leadership vacuum in the Army of Northern Virginia and had dealt a severe blow to Confederate morale. Douglas Southall Freeman notes in *Lee's Lieutenants: A Study in Command* that by summer 1862, "magic had become associated with the name of Jackson."[54] He had become a hero in the South for his brave battlefield exploits and his gentlemanly manner. His deep religious convictions endeared him to the public. His aggressiveness on the field and decisive action in combat similarly earned him the respect of his men and of Lee.

At the Battle of Chancellorsville on May 2, 1863, Jackson was on late night reconnaissance with his officers when his own sentries opened fire on the group, mistaking them for a Union ambush. Jackson was wounded and his left arm later amputated. The South would go on to win the battle, but as Lee noted, "Any victory is dearly brought which deprives us of the services of General Jackson, even for a short time."[55]

Jackson recovered smoothly and hoped to be back on the field within a month, but then he contracted pneumonia. Jackson's condition steadily worsened. Suffering bouts of delirium, he died on May 12, 1863. The Confederacy was wracked with grief. The *Richmond Examiner* wrote, "His extraordinary ability . . . is a power to the republic, and the loss . . . would be ill replaced by the accession of 50,000 troops to our present force."[56]

Without an adequate replacement to complement the loss of his most valued subordinate, Lee was at a serious disadvantage. Furthermore, his expedition had put him in unfamiliar territory, and he relied on Major General J.E.B. Stuart to provide him with valuable

Gettysburg: The Costliest Confederate Defeat

The blow delivered to Lee's army at Gettysburg was the worst the Confederate forces suffered in any single battle of the Civil War, with 37 percent of his men killed, wounded, or captured. Stephen W. Sears illustrates the damage in *Gettysburg*:

> General Lee recrossed the Potomac on July 13–14 with just under two-thirds of the men who had marched north across the river with him in June. The Confederate toll for the three days of Gettysburg came to 22,625, including 4,536 dead. Casualties on the march north, and on the retreat to Williamsport, added just over 4,500, raising the total for the campaign to some 27,125 men.

> Damage to the officer corps was severe. . . . Of the officers heading the army's forty-six divisional and brigade infantry commands at Gettysburg, nineteen were casualties.

> Losses among the field officers were severe as well, and in the most heavily engaged brigades, murderously so. . . . All told, of 171 infantry regiments, 78 (46 percent) suffered command casualties.

In May 1863, General Robert E. Lee ordered the Confederate army to invade the North, a maneuver that proved very costly for Lee's troops.

information on Union troop movements. Stuart's failure to report for several days forced Lee to engage the enemy without adequate knowledge of the placement or size of its force. His final frontal assault, led by Major General George Pickett and argued against by General Longstreet, ended in disaster, with Pickett's division utterly decimated. By the time the Army of Northern Virginia retreated into Confederate territory, it had lost ninety-seven officers and over twenty-two thousand men. Lee had only succeeded in exhausting his army, which would never fully recover from the defeat. Southern confidence in Lee's abilities was considerably shaken by the catastrophe at Gettysburg. The *Charleston Mercury* noted in the aftermath, "It is impossible for an invasion to have been more foolish and disastrous."[57]

Now the cost of Lee's refusal to send reinforcements to Pemberton at Vicksburg became all too apparent. Vicksburg fell to Grant on July 4, dealing another significant blow in the West, where Confederate fortunes had deteriorated continuously since 1862.

The Failure of the Army of Tennessee

Vicksburg was but one in a long list of disappointments suffered in the West. The Army of Tennessee had been the principal Confederate force there for a number of reasons. Tennessee was a vital state, supplying more army recruits than any other state after Virginia. It was also a major supplier of horses, mules, beef, pork, and grain. The city of Chattanooga was considered the strategic heart of the western Confederacy and the gateway to the Deep South because of the numerous railroad and river routes that ran through the city. Poor commanders and rampant personnel changes, however, led to the army's failure to fulfill its mission of defending the state from Union occupation.

Of the nine men who commanded the Army of Tennessee over the course of the war, Bragg served longer than any other general. Yet that experience failed to translate into significant Southern victories. Bragg, although he was considered a master at drilling his troops, proved a failure at commanding them in combat. In more than one battle, his reliance on close-order linear formations left his troops open to devastating federal fire, and he refused to develop alternative field strategies. Under his guidance, the army won only one battle, at Chickamauga, and there the South suffered two thousand more casualties than the Union forces. Only the withdrawal of the Union troops to nearby

Chattanooga allowed Bragg to claim this indecisive engagement as a victory. One of his officers noted, "All confidence in General Bragg is lost, and I do not believe this army can win a victory under his superintendence."[58] The army's fortunes would not improve after his relief.

Joseph Johnston, who initially resisted replacing Bragg, took command on December 16, 1863, but did little to improve the situation. He lost the Tennessee capital in Nashville after failing to provide an adequate defense and was driven clear into Georgia in the summer of 1864 by Sherman's troops as they fought their way toward Atlanta. Since Johnston rarely communicated his movements and intentions, Davis could not be certain if he intended to defend Atlanta. Finally, when Johnston admitted that he did not, Davis relieved him and placed John Bell Hood in command. Hood, with his back to the city, was too late to prevent Sherman's advance and was forced to abandon Atlanta on September 1, 1864. Hood's broken army moved south to avoid capture, then swung around Sherman and returned to Tennessee.

Andrew Haughton notes in *Training, Tactics and Leadership in the Confederate Army of Tennessee: Seeds of Failure,* "The training and tactics of the Army of Tennessee were weaknesses which constantly inhibited the potential of the Confederate forces and contributed to its miserable performance on a dozen battlefields from Shiloh to Nashville."[59] The failures of the Army of Tennessee also resulted in the loss of vital resources and territory to the Union.

The Withering Confederate Army

Defeats like Gettysburg and even victories like the one at Chickamauga severely depleted Confederate forces, reducing their ability to halt the steady Union advance into Southern territory. Military historians estimate that during the war, 198,000 Southern soldiers died of wounds suffered in battle, disease, starvation, and as prisoners of war, with an additional 137,000 wounded. While total Union casualties of 630,000 far exceed this number, Confederate losses amounted to fully one-third of its fighting force, a much higher comparative toll.

The South also suffered the loss of seventy-four battlefield generals, further compromising their ability to mount a sustained de-

Camp Douglas: To Die in Chicago

Union armies placed over two hundred thousand Confederate prisoners in prison camps during the Civil War. The prison at Camp Douglas, a few miles south of Chicago, had the highest mortality rate of all camps in the Union's penal system. Of the eighteen thousand Southerners interned there during the war, it is estimated that between forty-five hundred and six thousand died.

Over seventy thousand cases of pneumonia, bronchitis, scurvy, dysentery, and other diseases were recorded between February 1862 and June 1865. Punishment of the prisoners was also notoriously harsh. Survivors of the camp are quoted in George Levy's *To Die in Chicago: Confederate Prisoners at Camp Douglas, 1862–1865*:

> "The Yanks have fixed a frame near the gate . . . with a [beam] across it edge up, and about four feet from the ground, which they make our men ride whenever the men do anything that does not please them. It is called the Mule. Men have sat on it till they fainted and fell off. It is like riding a sharp top fence."

> "Another [punishment] was to make the men pull down their pants and sit, with nothing under them, on the snow and frozen ground. . . . When they got weary of this, they commenced whipping, making the men lay on a barrel, and using their belts, which had a leaden clasp with sharp edge . . . every lick inflicted thus cut entirely through the skin."

fense of Confederate territory. The loss of ranking general Albert Sidney Johnston and Thomas "Stonewall" Jackson, who was, at the time of his death, the South's most beloved commander, were among many that hampered the Confederate effort.

In time, Lee would replace Jackson as the hero of the South, but the high esteem of the people would not protect him from defeat. Lee's Army of Northern Virginia, ninety thousand strong when he took command in June 1862, had shrunk to just under ten thousand armed men when he surrendered to Grant at Appomattox, bringing an end to the war and the Confederate States of America.

The Moral Poverty of Slavery

Chapter 4

Perhaps the great and long-suppressed guilt over slavery, and the undeniable reality that the system was not as benevolent as most Southerners wanted to believe, required some sober reassessment of war aims and justification.

Herman Hattaway and Richard E. Berringer,
Jefferson Davis, Confederate President

D URING THE CIVIL War, many Southerners might have believed they were fighting for states' rights, but in practice that most often translated as the right to own slaves. More than just the prime factor in the call of secession, slavery was linked to the national identity and political culture of the Confederate States of America. Proponents of slavery firmly believed that any attempt to destroy or in any way alter the institution of slavery would bring down the nation. To prevent this, slaveholders mounted a vigorous defense of their way of life, relying on religion, racist ideology, and pseudoscientific evolutionary theories to support their case.

Yet this inflexible commitment to slavery placed a significant strain on the war effort by sapping manpower and food resources to control and feed the large slave population. It also deprived the Confederacy of moral legitimacy in the eyes of other nations who believed the South's attachment to a barbaric institution was worthy of neither recognition nor support. These factors played a part in the shifting of attitudes in the South away from traditional slavery, but the scattered calls for reform and even abolition of slavery came too late and too infrequently to save either Southerners' beloved institution or their nation.

In Defense of Degradation

"Your fathers and my fathers built this government on two ideas," declared Alabama fire-eater William L. Yancey in 1860. "The first is that the white race is the citizen, and the master race, and the white man is the equal of every other white man. The second idea is that the Negro is the inferior race."[60]

Yancey's white supremacist view was common to Southern thinking and at the center of the ideology that developed around slavery

Feeding and housing large numbers of slaves like these placed a tremendous strain on the Confederacy's limited wartime resources.

prior to the Civil War. For several decades after the nation's founding, the institution of slavery had been accepted in both the North and the South, the exception being the abolitionist movement rooted in the religious and cultural aristocracy based mainly in New England. However, after the fall of Fort Sumter, Southerners were motivated to further justify their beliefs, not only to differentiate their culture from that of the North but also to remind themselves of why they were fighting.

An entire literature and school of thought arose that defined blacks as savages incapable of caring for themselves, therefore justifying slavery as a means of civilizing them. By accepting the inferiority of the black race, white Southerners believed they were actually helping them improve their lot by holding them in bondage. Upon seeing her slaves freed by the Union Confiscation Act, for example, one Louisiana woman told federal troops, "Let the Negroes be. They are happier in their present state than they will be in their so called free one."[61] Whites could not accept the fact that slaves hated being held in bondage. That denial, in turn, was essential to the maintenance of slavery's ideology.

Far from countering this willful ignorance, the spiritual convictions held by white Southerners worked to blind them to the moral poverty of slavery. Pro-slavery preachers, in their sermons, suggested that slavery was not only ordained by God, but that it was impossible to live a moral life without the enforcement of racial hierarchy provided by slavery. Southerners were led to believe that the natural mastery of whites over blacks was part of God's order.

At the same time white preachers sought to convince slaves that their lot in life was ordained by God and that freedom was a tool of the devil. The hypocrisy of these sermons was evident to many slaves, however. One Fauquier County, Virginia, slave, for example, resisted his wife's pleas to join the church. "How can Jesus be just, if He will allow such oppression and wrong? How can God be just, when He not only permits, but sanctions such conduct?"[62]

Slave owners, however, still had to convince the two-thirds of white Southerners who did not own slaves that they had a stake in maintaining slavery. They constantly reminded nonslaveholders that without slavery they would be at the mercy of freed blacks who would overrun the land, attend white schools and churches, and take white men's jobs.

The Teachings of J.D.B. DeBow

J.D.B. DeBow, editor of the *New Orleans Review,* was one of the foremost proponents of the philosophy of slavery. He often filled the pages of his *Review* with essays explaining the moral rightness of human bondage. Some of his ideas are quoted in William C. Davis's *Look Away! A History of the Confederate States of America:*

> Everybody knows that slavery finds justification and authority throughout the whole of the Old and New Testaments, and that the Devil himself could not "find Scripture for his purpose," if the Devil be an abolitionist.

> All free society must reject the Bible if it approve its own institutions and disapprove slavery, because slavery is not only instituted and justified by the Christian God, but, much more, *"because Christian morality can be practiced only in slave society."*

> He who punishes his Negroes when they deserve it, and retains them in slavery, treating them humanely, fulfills the golden rule.

At the same time, slave owners contended that work once done by blacks would now have to be done by whites, reducing them to the status of peasants.

A Georgia editor noted that slavery made "the poor man respectable," giving him "an elevated position in society that they would not otherwise have." [63] Whites too poor to own slaves themselves often did support slavery because it gave them someone to look down upon. Even at their most desperate—living in poverty and subsisting on scraps of food—they could still say they were better than blacks. This led one pro-slavery Louisianan to proclaim, "Demagogues [what Southerners called abolitionists] can never array the poor against the rich upon the subject of slavery." [64]

This bold statement did not hold up in the face of disaffection that developed among poor whites over the Twenty Slave Law and other exemptions that kept slave owners out of the war. In fact, like slaves, poor whites suffered from the prejudices of a planter aristocracy that believed them to be destined to endure their lowly economic status forever. In the eyes of the rich, the needs of poor whites were secondary to their own.

The reality that black slaves and poor whites shared in being exploited worked against the wealthy planters. It was not uncommon for poor white families to hide runaway slaves, for example, or for slaves to provide temporary shelter for army deserters in their quarters on the plantations. Some whites recognized early on that slavery was working against the Confederacy in some areas. One of Governor Brown's followers noted shortly after Georgia seceded in February 1861, "The results of the late election for delegates in the mountains does not only indicate the Union sentiment, but more and worse, anti-[black] slavery!"[65]

Practical Problems of the Peculiar Institution

Once the war began, slaveholders found themselves in the odd position of fearing the very people that they were fighting to keep enslaved.

The flight of slaves increased as the war progressed. Nearly forty thousand escaped from Southern bondage in 1863.

Despite efforts by whites to keep knowledge of events from them, slaves realized that a Northern victory in the war would lead to their freedom. Planters further feared that each new Union victory increased the possibility of slave insurrection.

Fearing slave uprisings, communities across the South like Lowndes County, Georgia, called for stricter enforcement of laws that regulated the travel and congregation of slaves, "deem[ing] it indispensable to the protection of property."[66] Confederate home guards were formed, drawing tens of thousands of troops away from the front in the process.

The home guards, however, proved to be of little comfort or practical use, consisting as they did mainly of poor whites who had little stake or interest in their duties. Slave patrols made up of otherwise eligible conscripts who avoided fighting were also open to corruption and lawless behavior. Some planters and merchants bribed these patrols, ensuring lax enforcement of the laws that they claimed interfered with commerce. They continued to allow their slaves to travel and sell goods at market. As a result, the laws restricting the movements of slaves were only sporadically enforced, and slave owners caught in violation were rarely punished.

Still, slaves, because they were so close to their masters, were an ever-present threat. They aided Union soldiers who escaped from Confederate prisons and performed various acts of sabotage on equipment and crops. Field hands who did escape often acted as federal spies, providing valuable information on troop movements and supply routes. Runaway slaves, referred to in the North as contraband, also joined Union forces.

The flight of slaves became a more common phenomenon as the war progressed. Urged on by the spreading presence of the Union troops, slaves broke free at first in small numbers but later in droves. In Virginia, for example, there were 117 recorded runaways in 1860. In 1863, 37,706 slaves escaped in spite of increased patrols, the Confederate army, and the state militia. One planter remarked, "Negroes are constantly going off, and I doubt if 100 will be left [in the county] by the winter if the enemy remains."[67]

As the war progressed, slaves became more of a burden than a benefit for many Southerners. Food was scarce, and what few crops planters could grow went to their own slaves while the Confederate army subsisted on half and quarter rations. One Virginia woman renounced her slaves. "May the Yankeys take every Negro & do what they please with them." [68] Furthermore, as slave owners fled before invading Union troops they would bring their slaves with them, further straining the already inadequate food supplies. Still, many in the South continued to cling to slavery in the stubborn belief that human bondage was a workable institution.

In Vain Hope of Legitimacy

Such insistence on retaining slavery kept the Confederacy from earning the legitimacy it sought from other nations. Since the early days of the Confederacy, many in the South believed that independence would be assured if their sovereignty was formally recognized by other nations. Confederate diplomats actively sought recognition and support for their cause in Europe, but slavery proved an insurmountable stumbling block to their efforts. As Duncan Andrew Campbell noted in his study, *English Public Opinion and the American Civil War,* "No subject impacted upon the debate regarding the conflict across the ocean more than did slavery." [69]

The major focus of the South's pursuit of diplomatic recognition was Great Britain. At the time, England was the world's largest naval power and had the ships to break the Union's naval blockade of the South if it chose to do so. Also, the South's diplomats hoped that if England granted diplomatic recognition, France, Germany, and other countries would follow suit.

Despite Queen Victoria's proclamation of neutrality on May 5, 1861, Davis hoped that Britain would eventually abandon that stance. On the one hand, Davis thought he could exploit anti-American sentiment among the English to the South's gain. On the other hand, the Southern planters felt a strong kinship with the British aristocracy, thinking themselves courtly, in the manner of English country gentlemen.

These assumptions proved disastrously wrong. The British felt no connection to the Confederacy and thought its people were uncultured because they owned slaves. This view was reflected in the March 2, 1861, edition of the *Economist,* which stated that Southerners "seem actually to have no scruples, and their morality on all points seems to have been strangely warped by slavery."[70]

Southern diplomats similarly misread British relations with the Union. The British attitude toward America was one of annoyance rather than animosity. England may have been unsettled by American territorial expansion across the North American continent, but the British accepted it as long as there was no direct conflict with their own imperial ambitions. In fact, many British politicians worried that if England aided the Confederacy in securing its independence, the Union would retaliate, possibly by seizing Canada, which was still a British possession, as compensation for the loss of the South.

Union diplomats did their best to keep such fears alive. The skillful diplomacy of Union secretary of state William Seward kept the British guessing as to the potential Union reaction should England aid the South. Another American, Ambassador to Russia Cassius Clay, also wrote what was widely interpreted as a veiled threat in the May 20, 1861, edition of the London *Times:* "Is England so secure in the

---

 ## Black Slave Owners

Slavery was overwhelmingly, but not exclusively, a white institution. Throughout the South, there were free blacks who were themselves slave owners. Some black slave owners owned members of their own families, ensuring their protection from abuse. Others unscrupulously profited from the plight of their people. Black slave owners, however, were not viewed as having the same privileges or respect of white slave owners. Ervin L. Jordan Jr. explains in *Black Confederates and Afro-Yankees in Civil War Virginia:*

> One free black at Harper's Ferry purchased his wife and children . . . but his former master refused to sell the eldest daughter. . . . Another Afro-Virginian father in the town worked and saved $1,000 to buy his family only to have Confederate soldiers steal his money. Alexander Dunlop of Williamsburg paid $450 for his wife and $700 for her sister; afterward he was told he could not set them free. Another free black, Aggie Peters, bought her and her husband's freedom and went north. Upon her return to Virginia, she was arrested and "examined" by judges who banished her back to the North with a warning that if she were ever caught in the state again she would be whipped and sold.

---

future against home revolt or foreign ambition . . . to plant the seeds of revenge in all our future?"[71]

British response to Confederate requests for recognition and aid were not entirely dictated by fears of Union reprisal. England itself had outlawed slavery in 1833, though as much for economic reasons as for humanitarian ones. Nonetheless, working-class British citizens had grown to despise the institution and were loath to become reacquainted with it on any level.

Confederate diplomats James Mason and William Yancey were oblivious to the British public's hatred of slavery. The two envoys spent much of their time among Britain's wealthy aristocrats and incorrectly

Despite the British public's hatred of slavery, Southern diplomats James Mason (left) and William Yancey solicited support for the Confederacy among the British aristocracy.

assumed that their opinions reflected those of the nation in general. The aristocrats of Europe were eager to see the American democratic experiment fail because of their disdain for the lower classes, but this selfish sentiment was far outweighed by the broader public's revulsion to slavery. Yancey finally came to realize this and returned home on March 17, 1863. He reported to Davis, "The feeling against slavery in England is so strong that no public man there dares to extend a hand to help us." [72]

Events in the war itself eventually ended all hope of British, and consequently European, recognition and support of the Confederacy. Lincoln's Emancipation Proclamation of January 1, 1863, demonstrated to England that the war was not simply aimed at restoring the Union but was being waged to free the slaves, a cause the British would not oppose. Also, the twin defeats at Gettysburg and Vicksburg illustrated that the South's quest for independence was unlikely to succeed. Recognizing that the Confederacy's hopes for international recognition would not be realized, Davis called his diplomats home. He told the South, "Put not your trust in princes, and rest not your hopes on foreign nations. This war is ours; we must fight it out ourselves." [73]

Shifting Attitudes

Lincoln's Emancipation Proclamation imparted a moral element to the war, not just in the eyes of foreigners but for Northerners as well. Even in the South, although the "Insurrection Proclamation," as it was derisively called, was widely ignored, its psychological impact was significant. Mississippi Confederate congressman Henry C. Chambers reflected the rampant fear of Southerners months before when he noted, "Emancipation would be the destruction of our social and political system." [74]

Regardless of the North's position, Southerners themselves were increasingly concerned about the continued viability of slavery. The rise in slave disobedience and escapes made it clear that the institution as it had existed could not last. Changes would have to be made.

These changes were motivated in large part by a growing sense that slavery, far from being ordained by God (as Christian ministers had earlier preached), was in fact causing the South to lose God's favor. The continued and increasing hardships of war, Southerners began to believe, meant that God's wrath was now upon them. Still, few in the South argued that God directly opposed slavery. Instead, men like Presbyterian minister Robert Lewis Dabney asserted that God's disfavor was brought on by not allowing slaves to read the Bible. Lack of widespread Sabbath worship among slaves and a failure to give slave marriages legal recognition were also blamed.

The slave reform movement acted to address these issues and more practical concerns like preventing abuse and teaching slaves to read and write. It was believed that better treatment of slaves would prevent rebellion, a prospect that seemed all the more likely since the majority of able-bodied white men were away at war. Consequently, these changes were a means not of improving the lot of slaves but of ensuring the survival of the Confederacy. Yet, with mounting military setbacks depleting the armies, survival was in doubt. Bolder steps would need to be taken.

The Debate over Slave Enlistment

In the end, slavery came to be seen not as an institution worth fighting for but as something that could no longer be defended. General Joseph Johnston first entertained the idea of enlisting slaves in the Confederate army after witnessing the performance of black Union troops fighting in Tennessee in 1863. Davis at first resisted the idea but warmed to it after realizing that the South was running out of conscription-age white men. He submitted a proposal to the Confederate Congress in 1864 that offered compensation to slave owners whose slaves were enlisted in the army. The slaves would then be set free after dutiful completion of their military service.

The slave-owning aristocracy overwhelmingly opposed enlistment of what they considered their property. Although slaves already performed all manner of laborious tasks for the military, giving them the opportunity to fight and earn their freedom was altogether different. To the slave owners, this was a betrayal of Southern ideals. Robert Barnwell Rhett expressed this uncompromising view in the *Charleston Mercury*. "We are fighting for our system of civilization. We intend to fight for that, or nothing."[75]

Davis embraced a more pragmatic approach and worked to gain supporters for his cause. His war aim had initially been to secure slavery and independence for the South. After 1864, however, it had become apparent that either slavery or independence could be had, but not both. One of his correspondents noted in a February 1865 letter, "The teachings of Providence . . . dictate conclusively and emphatically that to secure and perpetuate our independence we must emancipate the Negro."[76]

Resignation to the fate of slavery took hold in many areas of the South. Mississippi congressman John T. Lamkin supported conscription, noting, "Slavery is played out whether we win or lose."[77] General Howell Cobb said, "If slaves will make good soldiers, our whole theory of slavery is wrong."[78] Even the combative *Richmond Examiner* admitted, "If a Negro is fit to be a soldier, he is not fit to be a slave."[79]

Whatever boost in manpower slaves might have given to Southern ranks, the initiative came too late. By the time the bill calling for slave

The Slavery Reform Movement

By the final months of the Confederacy, it was becoming apparent to slavery's supporters that judicious changes would need to be made if the institution was to survive. Reverend James Lyons of Mississippi outlined several reforms in a pamphlet he published February 11, 1865, entitled *On Slavery and the Duties Growing Out of the Relations*. William C. Davis, in *Look Away! A History of the Confederate States of America*, explains:

> Lyons made it clear that *"reformation,* and not *emancipation* is the duty of the South." . . . He called for legislatures to repeal their laws prohibiting slaves from being taught to read, to legalize slave marriages, to grant legal parental status to slave couples so that their children could not be sold away from them before the age of twelve, and to give better protection of slaves from the assaults of "low, vicious white men" by allowing slaves to testify in court in cases against their abusers. . . .

> "With these reforms, together with religious instruction, which must be enforced by *moral,* not *legal* means, slavery would be what the Bible recognizes," said Lyons, "and would be divested of its obnoxious features."

enlistment passed on March 13, 1865, the Confederate army, and the Confederacy itself, was in its final days. Some historians have speculated that if the debate over slave enlistment and emancipation had come to a logical conclusion sooner, the South might have stood a better chance at gaining its independence. As it happened, however, too many planters and pro-slavery politicians took the position that they would rather lose the war than give up slavery; as a consequence, they ended up doing both at once.

The Crumbling Cotton Kingdom

Chapter 5

We are an agrarian people; we are a primitive people. We have no cities—we don't want them. We have no literature—we don't need any. We have no press—we are glad of it. . . . We have no commercial maritime—no navy—we don't want them. We are better without them.

Louis T. Wigfall, quoted in *Lifeline of the Confederacy,* by Stephen R. Wise

O NE OF THE MOST significant factors in determining a nation's fortunes in war is the condition of its economy. This was no less true of the Confederacy during the Civil War. With a high concentration of its resources devoted to agricultural production, chiefly cotton, the Confederacy lacked the industrial capacity necessary to supply its armies and sustain its civilian population. The successful transition to a wartime economy was further impeded by shortages in labor and capital, and the lack of an adequate rail system with which to transport goods and materials.

The Confederate economy, and in turn the war effort, was also a victim of bad fiscal management by the government. Confederate currency was printed with abandon and plummeted in value, while the scarcity of goods drove prices far beyond the reach of the average Southerner. The Confederate government also mismanaged its primary export, choosing to horde cotton rather than ship it to Europe and establish a desperately needed source of foreign credit. By the time Confederate officials realized their error, a Union naval blockade had rendered the one export that the South's entire economy revolved around useless. All of the Confederacy's subsequent attempts to shore up its crumbling Cotton Kingdom met with disaster.

The Railroad Problem

To some historians, the outlook for the South was grim from the beginning and should have been obvious. J.D.B. DeBow, editor of the influential *New Orleans Review,* once noted, "We know of no surer indication of the wealth and enterprise of any people than the extent of their railways."[80] By this measure the South's prospects for victory were very slim indeed.

At the outbreak of the Civil War, of the thirty thousand miles of railroad track in America, approximately nine thousand miles of it was in the South. At least 113 different companies laid claim to what was largely a mismanaged, fragmented rail network that contained signif-

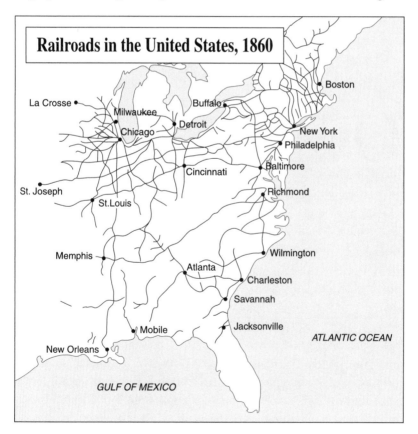

Railroads in the United States, 1860

Boston
La Crosse
Buffalo
Milwaukee
Detroit
Chicago
New York
Philadelphia
Cincinnati
Baltimore
St. Joseph
St.Louis
Richmond
Memphis
Wilmington
Atlanta
Charleston
Savannah
Jacksonville
Mobile
ATLANTIC OCEAN
New Orleans
GULF OF MEXICO

icant gaps between major cities and was wholly unsuited for the heavy use that war would bring. Many lines were not in strategically good positions for the movement of troops, and there were very few sidings to allow for the passage of trains traveling in opposite directions. There was no uniform gauge, or track width, in use throughout the system, so troops and supplies spent valuable time being transferred from one train to another instead of traveling straight through to their destination.

George Edgar Turner illustrates the extent of the problem in *Victory Rode the Rails:*

> Large areas of the Confederacy were far removed from rail transportation. In all of Texas, Arkansas, and Louisiana, only 700 miles of track were in operation. Much of the interior of Alabama and Mississippi was entirely without rail service, and from Lynchburg to Chattanooga, not a single line crossed the east-west trunk. In all the mountain area of North Carolina, east Tennessee, and southwestern Virginia, the only rail facilities other than the trunk line were three short spurs, the longest of which did not exceed twenty miles.[81]

The Confederate government was loath to get involved in imposing order on the rail network, and the owners and managers of the different lines were equally reluctant to concede control. The Confederate Congress did set up a system to regulate civilian and military use of trains, and placed the entire railway system under military command. This control existed mostly on paper, however, and was never fully put in force by the various officers placed in charge.

The government offered aid for the building of new lines and connections to close gaps in the network, and the railroad companies responded with a wide range of proposals, claiming each one to be of military necessity. The government attempted to discern which projects were the most pressing, but local politics and favoritism often skewed the selection process. Many of the approved projects were seriously delayed due to lack of resources or money, and some were never completed before the end of the war.

The shortage of railroads meant that of those that were in operation, some were run far harder than the equipment could tolerate. For example, the superintendent of the vital Virginia Central line reported,

"The locomotives are constantly used with loads to the extent of their capacity and cannot be spared for repairs; they are run until they can run no longer. Many of them are old and constantly out of order."[82]

The insufficient railroad system adversely affected the Southern war effort by impeding the flow of troops and supplies. Resources like coal, timber, and iron, which were vital to industry, and in particular, production of parts for railways, often failed to reach their destination because of distribution problems linked to the railroads.

Such distribution problems affected the cost of basic commodities as well. Prices varied widely because transportation problems led to an uneven distribution of supplies. For instance, in April 1864, corn that sold for $1.25 a bushel in Georgia sold for $40.00 in Richmond. That same month, Secretary of War James Seddon noted, "Of all the difficulties encountered by the administrative bureaus, perhaps the greatest has been the deficiency in transportation."[83]

Too Many Farms, but Too Little Food

The lack of railroads also proved a serious impediment to industrial development in the South, but at the start of the war, that was of little concern. For decades, the plantation system had provided a lucrative means of income. As a result an overwhelming portion of Southern resources were devoted to agricultural pursuits. The favorable climate and the abundance of slave labor created ideal conditions for producing cotton, a crop on which the South had become increasingly dependent for its income. Mark A. Weitz illustrates the situation in *A Higher Duty: Desertion Among Georgia Troops During the Civil War:*

> By 1860, the South's principal staple crops were rice, sugar, hemp, tobacco, and cotton. Before the war, wheat, corn and other grain crops had to come from the North's commercial agriculture system, which quadruped its food production in the forty years preceding the war. From 1850 to 1860, planters put every available acre into cotton.[84]

This reliance on imports for even basic food crops became a serious problem when the war cut off supplies from the North. The demands of feeding the Confederate army placed a great strain on existing agricultural resources. Foraging Union troops further de-

Salt Socialism

The economic hardships of war forced the Confederate states to abandon their traditional policy of noninvolvement in business and become extremely active in manufacturing and production. One commodity in dire need of management was salt, which was in short supply and highly valued as a food preservative. As William C. Davis notes in *Look Away! A History of the Confederate States of America,* the states met with varying degrees of success in this regard:

> In the fall of 1861, the Alabama legislature passed a bill outlawing monopolies in salt production, and further prohibited the commercial export of state-manufactured salt . . . in order to discourage speculation and profiteering.

> In neighboring Georgia at almost the same time the legislature authorized Governor Brown to seize all supplies of salt in the state, both that in the hands of outright speculators capitalizing on the increased demand on limited production and that belonging to legitimate merchants and manufacturers. There came an immediate outcry that law-abiding people suddenly could not buy a single sack of salt.

> In Florida, meanwhile, the legislature authorized Governor Milton to assume complete control of the state's salt supplies. . . . In desperation, by April 1862 people were forging the governor's signature on orders in order to get a few sacks from the warehouses, and when any fell into the hands of the unscrupulous, they quickly marketed it at extortionate prices.

pleted food crops, and as a result, many civilians suffered from starvation.

Eventually, planters were encouraged to grow corn in place of cotton. Few planters willingly switched, however, opting instead to cash in on the high prices cotton could earn on the black market. The Confederate government made the transition to food production compulsory in 1863, stigmatizing men like Robert Toombs who continued to refuse the noble pursuit of growing food to feed his fellow countrymen. In his own defense Toombs responded, "Let them take up arms and come with me to drive the invader from our soil and then we will settle what sort of seeds shall be put in it."[85]

The prewar dependence on imports extended to manufactured goods, many of which came from England and Europe and were cut off when the Union imposed a blockade of Southern ports. This forced the Confederacy to quickly develop the industrial base it had ignored for so many years. Despite being a mostly agricultural region, the South was not entirely helpless in this area and did have some factories that met production demands for much of the war. However, the Union possessed an industrial base that had produced 90 percent of the nation's manufactured goods in the year before the Civil War.

A principal barrier to the South's industrial makeover was a lack of skilled labor. Draft exemptions for machinists and metalworkers kept some valuable workers off the battlefield, but there were not enough of them to go around. Economist Victor S. Clark notes of this scarcity in *Economic Impact of the American Civil War,* "It seems to have been the limiting factor in the production of arms and munitions up to the very close of the conflict."[86] Other shortages in the materials of production—machines, machine parts, and iron ore—also hindered industrial development.

Many fledgling business ventures failed due to these shortages despite the intervention of state governments on their behalf. Southern businessmen were not schooled in industrial management and were prone to making costly production mistakes. They also suffered from a lack of capital; funds that might have gone toward nurturing manufacturing businesses were instead being invested in building ships to run the blockade. Many factories that did not close were eventually targeted by the invading Union armies, which, after 1864, made their seizure or destruction a priority.

The Cotton Fiasco

The South would pay a heavy price for its dependence on cotton as its principal source of income. In 1860, the South exported over 3 million bales, but the establishment of the Union blockade made it evident that this level was unlikely to continue. The Confederacy needed to find a way to capitalize on its signature product in spite of impending hardship.

Davis turned to what some historians have referred to as King Cotton diplomacy. This concept was based on the idea that cotton was so important to the nations of Europe that their ships would run the blockade, and these nations might even enter the war on the Confederacy's side in order to ensure its continued supply. With this in mind, Davis declared a cotton embargo and instructed his envoys to make certain

that "the British ministry will comprehend fully the condition to which
the British realm would be reduced if the supply of our staple should
suddenly fail or even be considerably diminished."[87] This plan was
ridiculed by Toombs and Vice President Stephens, who proposed instead sending as much cotton to England as possible and use it as a
means of establishing financial credit in Europe.

Davis, on the other hand, felt his policy would take advantage of
certain undeniable facts. England was the principal international cus-
tomer for the South's cotton, importing 78 percent of Southern planters'
1859 exports. For its part, Britain did seem extraordinarily dependent on Southern cotton. In 1860, the South supplied 85 percent of the
raw cotton purchased in the British city of Lancashire, the world's
largest manufacturing center for cotton products. The British textile

*Northern troops seize the cargo of a cotton ship during the Union blockade
of Southern ports. The blockade crippled the Confederate economy.*

industry, which employed nearly 5 million workers, clearly could not do without cotton.

Still, Davis's plan backfired. The year 1859 had seen a bumper cotton crop in the South, and British warehouses still stored enough of a surplus to supply the nation's mills for some time. The British also resented what they saw as blackmail by the Confederacy, particularly after they had already expressed their intent to remain neutral. The *Economist* noted on January 16, 1861, "Have South Carolina and Georgia really persuaded themselves that . . . England . . . should interfere in a struggle between the Federal Union and the revolted states . . . simply for the sake of buying their cotton at a cheaper rate?" [88]

British prime minister Lord Henry Palmerston did express pleasure at the idea of a cotton-producing Confederacy dedicated to free trade with Europe. Likewise, some British businessmen expressed the sentiment that England should break the Union blockade to get their cotton. However, a majority believed this would invite armed conflict with the Union and, therefore, was too high a price to pay. Instead, they turned to India, which was also a cotton-producing nation and, as a British colony, unlikely to cause the trouble that doing business with the South would incur.

Davis, through his own provincial beliefs, had misjudged the power of King Cotton. Even worse, he missed the only opportunity he would get to take advantage of Stephens's and Toombs's plan to ship cotton to England. The Union blockade grew steadily tighter with each passing week and would allow only four hundred thousand more bales of cotton to escape the South from 1862 through the end of the war.

The Blockade Exacts a Heavy Toll

The Northern blockade of the thirty-five-hundred-mile Southern coastline eventually isolated the Confederacy from much of the rest of the world. Initially, the forty-two-ship Union navy had only the resources to obstruct access to the principal ports of New Orleans, Mobile, and Charleston. Southerners were not alarmed at these developments, despite the early effect this had on the price of goods. A relative of Confederate general Howell Cobb asserted, "We can laugh at the blockade for a while if salt is $12 [instead of $2] per sack." [89] Less than a year later, however, salt sold for $125 per sack, when it was available at all.

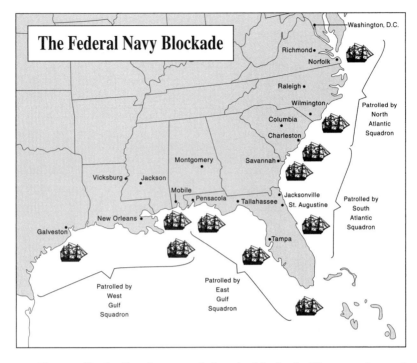

Eventually the South responded to the blockade. However, instead of working to boost its manufacturing capabilities, the South devoted more resources into running the blockade. The government enlisted the help of private companies like the Southern Steamship Company of New Orleans to build narrow, light ships that were fast enough to outrun or completely elude the Union ships and slip goods in and out of Confederate ports.

For a time the Confederate strategy worked. In 1861, the blockade-runners enjoyed great success, losing only one in ten cargoes to the Union. However, although blockade-running was a very lucrative operation that attracted millions of dollars in investments, the focus was on importing luxury goods for the planter aristocracy. Over time, as the Union navy expanded, it reduced the success rate of the blockade-runners, driving the price of imported goods higher. Desperately needed war materials and manufactured items from Europe arrived with greater infrequency, while cotton sat in warehouses, where it was in danger of being seized or burned by Union forces. By 1865, with the Union blockade numbering over five hundred ships, one in every two blockade-runners was seized or run aground. As a result, the products that could not be manufactured in the South became virtually impossible to obtain.

The Confederate Dollar Has No Value

The state of the Southern economy could not be exclusively blamed on blockade-induced shortages. Dreadful mismanagement of the Confederacy's monetary policy and its reckless printing of paper money brought more financial distress than any other single factor. As economist Eugene M. Lerner notes in *Economic Impact of the American Civil War,* "The money spent by the Confederate government to purchase war supplies came largely from the printing press; tax collections and bond sales raised relatively small amounts." [90]

The principal architect of this flawed policy was Treasury Secretary Christopher Memminger, a man whose marginal acquaintance with the economic theories of the time limited his effectiveness. His fellow politicians thought little of his abilities. Josiah Gorgas, head

---

 ## The Tax in Kind

On April 24, 1863, the Confederate government established a tax in kind consisting of one-tenth of the value of all farm produce, paid in the form of the produce itself. E. Merton Coulter explains the tax, and the problems it led to, in *The Confederate States of America, 1861–1865:*

> Those articles which must be shared with the government to the extent of one tenth were carefully enumerated: wheat, corn, oats, rye, "buckwheat or rice," sweet and Irish potatoes, hay and fodder, sugar, molasses, cotton, wool, tobacco, peas, beans, and ground peas. In order not to take the necessary foods from the farmers, each might reserve 50 bushels each of sweet potatoes, Irish potatoes, and wheat, 100 bushels of corn, and 20 bushels of either peas or beans. Also, each farmer must give ³⁄₅₀ of all pork, in the form of cured bacon. On all cattle, horses and mules not used in cultivation and all asses, he must pay a tax of one percent.

> But it was difficult to administer and left much bitterness among many small farmers who had never before paid a tax of any kind. It was not uniformly collected, as isolated districts went free of it while easily accessible regions made most of the contributions. Much material rotted at the depots or was stolen, and the whole system opened up wide possibilities for dishonesties by the quartermaster agents as well as by impostors.

---

of the Quartermaster Department, noted, "Mr. Memminger treats others with rudeness, and is, besides, dogmatical, narrow-minded and slow."[91]

Memminger failed to develop a coherent economic strategy for the Confederacy. He rejected establishing a broad income tax to generate revenue for the government, relying instead on a minor 0.5 percent tax on property, and most of the states borrowed money from the government to pay their share. Other schemes, such as the tax in kind, a tax of one-tenth of all farm produce, and foreign loans, met with limited success.

Memminger's solution to the cash crunch—printing more money—only drove down the value of the Confederate dollar. The stock of paper money increased elevenfold between 1861 and 1864. By that time it took $30 in Confederate paper to equal $1 in gold. The territory in which Confederate currency was even accepted continuously shrank as Union forces advanced. Moreover, many Southern lenders and merchants refused to deal in Confederate dollars, resorting to gold, silver, and even Union "greenbacks," as the currency of the Union was known. Additionally, Confederate dollars were easily counterfeited, and the government accepted the best renditions as legal tender, further ballooning the money supply.

The result of the printing of so much money, coupled with a scarcity of goods, resulted in runaway inflation, which also placed a heavy burden on the civilian population. Shoes went from $1.50 a pair to $15.00. Apples rose to $25.00 a bushel, and beef to $2.00 per pound. The weekly cost of feeding a family in Richmond rose from $6.55 in 1860 to $68.25 in 1863. As early as 1862, citizens and merchants in some areas resorted to bartering in edible goods or in gold, silver, and jewelry. For instance, the *Early County News* of Georgia sold one-year subscriptions in trade for eight pounds of bacon, lard, or sugar. Speculators who sold goods at top-dollar prices, or who hoarded them in hopes of earning a profit from rising prices, compounded the inflation problem. Davis condemned this practice, saying, "The passion of speculation has become a gigantic evil."[92] However, the establishment of price controls failed to keep inflation in check and did not address the larger issue of the excess supply of money.

Like all the other factors that played a significant role in the fall of the Confederacy, the poor management of the Southern economy created a spiral of crises that fed off each other. Inflated prices inspired speculation and hoarding of goods, which consequently increased demand and drove prices even higher. The printing of too much money drove down the value of Confederate currency, which in turn sparked the printing of even more money.

The case could even be made that the South's economic backwardness set the Confederacy on a course to defeat before the Union ever established its blockade. The lack of diversity of the Southern economy left the Confederates with no sound way to fund the war when they could no longer rely on King Cotton to save them. Their attempts to develop their industrial capacity and expand their railroad network during wartime stretched their limited manpower and financial resources to the breaking point. In order to compensate, they embarked on a string of poor decisions that only exacerbated their problems, contributing to the fall of the Confederacy.

Legacy of a Lost Cause

Epilogue

Not for fame or reward,
Not for place or for rank,
Not lured by ambition,
Or goaded by necessity,
But in Simple
Obedience to Duty
As they understood it,
These men suffered all,
Sacrificed all,
Dared all—and died.

Inscription on the monument to the dead
of the Confederate States Army, Arlington
National Cemetery, Washington, D.C.

ON APRIL 9, 1865, at the village known as Appomattox Courthouse, General Robert E. Lee, seeing the destruction of his forces as unavoidable, surrendered the Army of Northern Virginia to the overwhelmingly superior Union forces commanded by General Ulysses S. Grant. Lee's surrender signaled the end of the Civil War, although scattered fighting would continue for weeks, culminating in the complete cessation of hostilities by the end of May.

Days before the surrender, Jefferson Davis abandoned Richmond with what was left of his government and was on the run, hoping in vain to carry the fight for the South into the hills. That hope ended on

May 10, when he was captured in Georgia. Davis's wife, Varina, had given him her shawl to hide his face, and he was, therefore, subjected to wide ridicule for being caught wearing women's clothing. Davis was never formally charged with any crime but spent two years in jail before being released on bond.

Meanwhile, with news of Lee's surrender, Abraham Lincoln prepared for national reunification. He opted against harsh punishments for the Southern people and sought instead a peaceful reunion and rebuilding, as indicated in his second inaugural speech on March 4. "With malice toward none; with charity for all; with firmness in the right, as God gives us to see the right, let us strive on to finish the work

Dressed in his wife's clothes, Jefferson Davis is captured by Union soldiers in May 1865. One month earlier, General Lee surrendered at Appomattox, signaling the end of the Civil War.

we are in." [93] Lincoln did not live to see his work fulfilled. On April 15, John Wilkes Booth, an unemployed Southern actor seeking to avenge the Confederate defeat, fatally shot Lincoln as the president sat watching a play at Ford's Theatre in Washington, D.C. Booth was killed eleven days later by Union soldiers, and several of his accomplices were caught and after a brief trial were found guilty and hanged.

The succession of Vice President Andrew Johnson to the presidency ushered in the age of Reconstruction, a painful time in American history that led to widespread political corruption and extreme racial bitterness. The slaves were freed, made citizens, and guaranteed the right to vote by the Thirteenth, Fourteenth, and Fifteenth amendments to the U.S. Constitution. Yet African Americans faced a long, hard struggle before they could claim prosperity. Blacks suffered segregation, racism, and economic exploitation throughout the South, living in the shadow of their former masters and their descendants. A full century would pass before they achieved true legal equality in America, and the effects of hundreds of years of slavery and racist mistreatment continue to be felt even today.

The Confederate States of America: Doomed to Failure?

Some historians have expressed the belief that low morale alone brought about the Confederate defeat. Others have made the case that the fall of the Confederacy came on the battlefield, or by its own hand in the form of a steadfast adherence to states' rights. Of course, all these factors played a part in the destruction of the Confederate States of America, together with their inability to match a determined, industrialized enemy and their tragic attachment to the abhorrent institution of human slavery.

Another view that historians argue is that no single element could have brought doom on the Confederacy if the other elements had worked in its favor. According to this reasoning, a strong industrial base could have compensated for a weak military, and keener economic policies could have likewise balanced out the drop in public morale. With the commitment and resilience that Southerners had displayed in their cause immediately following secession, these historians surmise that nothing short of a wide array of complicated problems could have brought defeat.

The Death of Edmund Ruffin

Edmund Ruffin had been a farmer, an agricultural reformer, and a fire-eater in the days leading up to the Civil War, actively campaigning across the South for secession. As an honorary member of South Carolina's Palmetto Guard, he has been widely credited with firing the first shot at Fort Sumter in 1861. When his home state of Virginia seceded, Ruffin returned there and fought throughout the war. After Lee's surrender, Union soldiers freed his slaves, cut down all the trees on his plantation, and sowed salt across his fields to ruin the soil.

Unrepentant to the end, Ruffin viewed the coming peace and reunion with anger that gave way to dread. On June 18, 1865, he made his final diary entry, as quoted in Ervin L. Jordan Jr.'s *Black Confederates and Afro-Yankees in Civil War Virginia:*

> With death approaching near, I beg an humble grave for my mortal remains in the soil & among the patriotic & generous people of South Carolina. . . . I commit the care of my reputation & to them for a due appreciation [of my] zealous efforts to promote the best interests of Virginia.

That afternoon, Ruffin shot himself in the head.

In the final assessment, victory would belong to whoever desired it most and to whoever believed more strongly in their cause. It could not be the South, where, in the end, many came to realize the moral repugnance of slavery and no longer believed it worth supporting. But in the North, as Lincoln explained, it was "a struggle for maintaining in the world that form and substance of government whose leading object is to elevate the condition of men."[94]

This motivation proved stronger than any the South could offer and leaves open the discussion to explore one last reason for the great defeat of the Confederacy and the end of slavery—one expressed by Confederate major general George Pickett when he was asked to explain the failure of his charge at Gettysburg. He replied simply, "I think the Union army had something to do with it."[95]

Notes

Introduction: Moving Toward Conflict

1. Quoted in William Lee Miller, *Arguing About Slavery: The Great Battle in the United States Congress.* New York: Alfred A. Knopf, 1995, p. 123.
2. Quoted in Miller, *Arguing About Slavery,* p. 215.
3. Quoted in William C. Davis, *The Union That Shaped the Confederacy: Robert Toombs and Alexander Stephens.* Lawrence: University Press of Kansas, 2001, p. 68.
4. Quoted in Erik Bruun and Jay Crosby, eds., *Our Nation's Archive: The History of the United States in Documents.* New York: Black Dog & Leventhal, 1999, p. 324.
5. Quoted in Roy P. Basler, ed., *The Collected Works of Abraham Lincoln,* vol. 4. New Brunswick, NJ: Rutgers University Press, 1953, p. 263.
6. Quoted in Shelby Foote, *The Civil War: A Narrative: Fort Sumter to Perryville.* New York: Random House, 1958, p. 47.

Chapter 1: War Between the States: A Battle of Wills

7. Quoted in Foote, *The Civil War: A Narrative,* Vol. 1 p. 59.
8. David Herbert Donald, *Lincoln.* New York: Simon & Schuster, 1995, p. 311.
9. Clement Eaton, *A History of the Southern Confederacy.* New York: Macmillan, 1954, p. 89.
10. Foote, *The Civil War: A Narrative,* Vol. 1 p. 60.
11. Quoted in James M. McPherson, *Abraham Lincoln and the Second American Revolution.* New York: Oxford University Press, 1991, p. 26.
12. Quoted in Foote, *The Civil War: A Narrative,* Vol. 1 p. 65.

13. Quoted in Brian Steel Wills, *The War Hits Home: The Civil War in Southeastern Virginia.* Charlottesville: University of Virginia Press, 2001, p. 74.
14. Quoted in Thomas B. Buell, *The Warrior Generals: Combat Leadership in the Civil War.* New York: Crown, 1997, p. 130.
15. Quoted in Wills, *The War Hits Home,* p. 203.
16. Quoted in William C. Davis, *Look Away! A History of the Confederate States of America.* New York: Simon & Schuster, 2002, p. 171.
17. Quoted in Richard E. Berringer, Herman Hattaway, Archer Jones, and William N. Still Jr., *Why the South Lost.* Athens: University of Georgia Press, 1986, p. 435.
18. Eaton, *A History of the Southern Confederacy,* p. 8.
19. Quoted in Mark A. Weitz, *A Higher Duty: Desertion Among Georgia Troops During the Civil War.* Lincoln: University of Nebraska Press, 2000, p. 75.
20. Quoted in Ella Lonn, *Desertion During the Civil War.* Gloucester, MA: P. Smith, 1966, p. 29.
21. Quoted in George C. Rable, *The Confederate Republic: A Revolution Against Politics.* Chapel Hill: University of North Carolina Press, 1994, p. 287.

Chapter 2: Confederate Politics: Fighting the Union and Each Other

22. Quoted in Davis, *Look Away!* p. 331.
23. Quoted in Marshall C. DeRosa, *The Confederate Constitution of 1861.* Columbia: University of Missouri Press, 1991, p. 135.
24. Quoted in DeRosa, *The Confederate Constitution of 1861,* p. 99.
25. Quoted in E. Merton Coulter, *The Confederate States of America, 1861–1865.* Baton Rouge: Louisiana State University Press, 1950, p. 103.
26. Quoted in Herman Hattaway and Richard E. Berringer, *Jefferson Davis, Confederate President.* Lawrence: University Press of Kansas, 2002, p. 102.
27. Quoted in Eaton, *A History of the Southern Confederacy,* p. 49.
28. Quoted in Hattaway and Berringer, *Jefferson Davis, Condeferate President,* p. 32.

29. Thomas E. Schott, *Alexander H. Stephens of Georgia: A Biography.* Baton Rouge: Louisiana State University Press, 1988, p. 331.

30. Quoted in Schott, *Alexander H. Stephens of Georgia,* p. 407.

31. Quoted in Schott, *Alexander H. Stephens of Georgia,* p. 421.

32. Schott, *Alexander H. Stephens of Georgia,* p. 397.

33. Quoted in Eaton, *A History of the Southern Confederacy,* p. 263.

34. Quoted in Davis, *Look Away!* p. 337.

35. Quoted in Hattaway and Berringer, *Jefferson Davis, Confederate President,* p. 43.

36. Quoted in W. Buck Yearns, ed., *The Confederate Governors.* Athens: University of Georgia Press, 1985, p. 74.

37. Quoted in Shelby Foote, *The Civil War: A Narrative: Fredericksburg to Meridian.* New York: Random House, 1963, p. 649.

38. Quoted in Shelby Foote, *The Civil War: A Narrative: Red River to Appomattox.* New York: Random House, 1974, p. 93.

39. Coulter, *The Confederate States of America,* p. 402.

40. Quoted in Coulter, *The Confederate States of America,* p. 348.

41. Quoted in Archer Jones, *Civil War Command and Strategy.* New York: Free Press, 1992, p. 123.

Chapter 3: Flawed Military Leadership

42. Thomas L. Connelly and Archer Jones, *The Politics of Command: Factions and Ideas in the Confederate Strategy.* Baton Rouge: Louisiana State University Press, 1973, p. 186.

43. Connelly and Jones, *The Politics of Command,* p. 46.

44. Quoted in Steven E. Woodworth, *Davis and Lee at War.* Lawrence: University Press of Kansas, 1995, p. 130.

45. Quoted in Steven E. Woodworth, *Jefferson Davis and His Generals: The Failure of Confederate Command in the West.* Lawrence: University Press of Kansas, 1990, p. 177.

46. Quoted in Foote, *The Civil War: A Narrative: Fort Sumter to Perryville,* p. 665.

47. Quoted in Hattaway and Berringer, *Jefferson Davis, Confederate President,* p. 32.

48. Quoted in Davis, *The Union That Shaped the Confederacy,* p. 143.

49. Buell, *The Warrior Generals,* p. 46

50. Quoted in Yearns, *The Confederate Governors,* p. 152.

51. Quoted in Steven E. Woodworth, *No Band of Brothers: Problems in the Rebel High Command.* Columbia: University of Missouri Press, 1999, p. 140.
52. Quoted in James A. Rawley, *Turning Points in the Civil War.* Lincoln: University of Nebraska Press, 1966, p. 11.
53. Quoted in Stephen W. Sears, *Gettysburg.* New York: Houghton Mifflin, 2003, p. 4.
54. Douglas Southall Freeman, *Lee's Lieutenants: A Study in Command,* vol. 1: *Manassas to Malvern Hill.* New York: Charles Scribner's Sons, 1942, p. 303.
55. Quoted in Foote, *The Civil War: A Narrative: Fredericksburg to Meridian,* p. 316.
56. Quoted in Douglas Southall Freeman, *Lee's Lieutenants: A Study in Command,* vol. 2: *Cedar Mountains to Chancellorsville.* New York: Charles Scribner's Sons, 1943, p. 683.
57. Quoted in Foote, *The Civil War: A Narrative: Fredericksburg to Meridian,* p. 641.
58. Quoted in Andrew Haughton, *Training, Tactics and Leadership in the Confederate Army of Tennessee: Seeds of Failure.* London: Frank Cass, 2000, p. 121.
59. Haughton, *Training, Tactics and Leadership,* p. 182.

Chapter 4: The Moral Poverty of Slavery

60. Quoted in McPherson, *Abraham Lincoln and the Second American Revolution,* p. 50.
61. Quoted in Stephen V. Ash, *When the Yankees Came: Conflict and Chaos in the Deep South, 1861–1865.* Chapel Hill: University of North Carolina Press, 1995, p. 157.
62. Quoted in Ervin L. Jordan Jr., *Black Confederates and Afro-Yankees in Civil War Virginia.* Charlottesville: University of Virginia Press, 1995, p. 106.
63. Quoted in Coulter, *The Confederate States of America,* p. 10.
64. Quoted in Rable, *The Confederate Republic,* p. 81.
65. Quoted in David Williams, Teresa Crisp Williams, and David Carlson, *Plain Folk in a Rich Man's War: Class and Dissent in Confederate Georgia.* Gainesville: University of Florida Press, 2000, p. 133.

66. Quoted in Williams, Williams, and Carlson, *Plain Folk in a Rich Man's War,* p. 137.
67. Quoted in Ash, *When the Yankees Came,* p. 153.
68. Quoted in Ash, *When the Yankees Came,* p. 224.
69. Duncan Andrew Campbell, *English Public Opinion and the American Civil War.* Woodbridge, Suffolk, UK: Boydell, 2003, p. 18.
70. Quoted in Campbell, *English Public Opinion and the American Civil War,* p. 47.
71. Quoted in Campbell, *English Public Opinion and the American Civil War,* p. 33.
72. Quoted in Philip Van Doren Stern, *When the Guns Roared: World Aspects of the Civil War.* Garden City, NY: Doubleday, 1965, p. 112.
73. Quoted in Foote, *The Civil War: A Narrative: Fredericksburg to Meridian,* p. 655.
74. Quoted in Rable, *The Confederate Republic,* p. 288.
75. Quoted in Davis, *Look Away!* p. 160.
76. Quoted in Berringer, Hattaway, Jones, and Still, *Why the South Lost,* p. 373.
77. Quoted in Hattaway and Berringer, *Jefferson Davis, Confederate President,* p. 346.
78. Quoted in Eaton, *A History of the Southern Confederacy,* p. 276.
79. Quoted in Berringer, Hattaway, Jones, and Still, *Why the South Lost,* p. 386.

Chapter 5: The Crumbling Cotton Kingdom

80. Quoted in Robert C. Black, *The Railroads of the Confederacy.* Chapel Hill: University of North Carolina Press, 1952, p. 1.
81. George Edgar Turner, *Victory Rode the Rails.* Indianapolis, IN: Bobbs-Merrill, 1953, p. 32.
82. Quoted in Turner, *Victory Rode the Rails,* p. 239.
83. Quoted in Black, *The Railroads of the Confederacy,* p. 225.
84. Weitz, *A Higher Duty,* p. 128.
85. Quoted in Davis, *The Union That Shaped the Confederacy,* p. 164.
86. Quoted in Ralph Andreano, ed., *Economic Impact of the American Civil War.* Cambridge, MA: Schenkman, 1967, p. 43.
87. Quoted in Hattaway and Berringer, *Jefferson Davis, Confederate President,* p. 50.

88. Quoted in Campbell, *English Public Opinion and the American Civil War,* p. 51.
89. Quoted in Williams, Williams, and Carlson, *Plain Folk in a Rich Man's War,* p. 34.
90. Quoted in Andreano, *Economic Impact of the American Civil War,* p. 31.
91. Quoted in Eaton, *A History of the Southern Confederacy,* p. 235.
92. Quoted in Paul W. Gates, *Agriculture and the Civil War.* New York: Alfred A. Knopf, 1965, p. 44.

Epilogue: Legacy of a Lost Cause

93. Quoted in Foote, *The Civil War: A Narrative: Red River to Appomattox,* p. 813.
94. Quoted in McPherson, *Abraham Lincoln and the Second American Revolution,* p. 29.
95. Quoted in Sears, *Gettysburg,* p. xiv.

Chronology

1804
By this year, all Northern states have abolished slavery.

1808
United States abolishes the slave trade.

1820
Missouri Compromise prohibits slavery above latitude 36° 30' north in the Louisiana Purchase.

1844
Texas enters the Union as a slave state.

1848
United States wins the Mexican War, acquires territory referred to as Mexican Cession connecting Texas to California.

1850
Compromise of 1850—California enters Union as a free state, the slave trade in Washington, D.C., is abolished, and the Mexican Cession will determine slave status by popular sovereignty.

1854
Kansas-Nebraska Act repeals the Missouri Compromise and allows for imposition of slavery in the Kansas and Nebraska territories by popular sovereignty.

1857
Supreme Court rules in *Dred Scott v. Sandford* that slaves are property protected by the Constitution. The Missouri Compromise is also ruled unconstitutional.

1860
November: Abraham Lincoln elected president.

December 20: South Carolina secedes from the Union.

1861

January–March: Mississippi, Florida, Alabama, Georgia, Louisiana, and Texas secede.

February 4: Delegates from the seceded states gather in Montgomery, Alabama, to form Confederate States of America. They draw up a constitution and elect Jefferson Davis president.

April 12: Fort Sumter, South Carolina, is attacked by Confederate forces. It falls two days later. War begins.

April–June: Lincoln's call for seventy-five thousand volunteers sparks the secession of Virginia, Arkansas, North Carolina, and Tennessee.

May 5: Britain proclaims neutrality in war. Confederates continue scheming to draw Britain in on the South's behalf.

May 16: Confederate general staff appointed. In rank order: Samuel Cooper, Albert Sidney Johnston, Robert E. Lee, Joseph E. Johnston, P.G.T. Beauregard.

July 21: Battle of Manassas, also known as Bull Run. Confederate victory.

September 4: Confederate forces march into neutral Kentucky, sparking outrage. Kentucky joins the Union.

1862

February 27: Confederate Congress passes first act suspending habeas corpus in regions threatened by invasion.

April 16: First Confederate Conscription Act calls for all able-bodied men between eighteen and thirty-five to enlist in the army for three years.

June: Confederate Sequestration Act allows for seizure of alien property in the Confederacy, with proceeds to compensate planters for losses incurred by war.

June 1: Robert E. Lee appointed commanding general of the Army of Northern Virginia.

July 17: Union Confiscation Act gives federal soldiers the power to seize any Confederate property, including slaves, that could be used to aid and comfort Southern war effort.

September 27: Confederate conscription raised to include all men eighteen to forty-five.

1863

January 1: Lincoln issues the Emancipation Proclamation, which frees the slaves.

March 17: Diplomat William Yancey returns from England, reports to Davis that slavery issue prevents British assistance.

May 2: "Stonewall" Jackson is accidentally wounded by his own sentries at the Battle of Chancellorsville. The Confederates win the battle, but Jackson dies ten days later.

July 1–3: Battle of Gettysburg. Lee's army sustain's twenty-two thousand casualties, including ninety-seven officers.

July 4: Vicksburg falls to Union forces, giving them control of the Mississippi River.

October 13: Confederate Congress passes second act suspending habeas corpus.

1864

February 15: Confederate Congress passes third act suspending habeas corpus.

February 17: Third conscription act expanded to include all men seventeen to fifty.

May–September: Atlanta campaign.

September 1: Hood abandons Atlanta.

September–December: Sherman's march to the sea.

1865

January 26: Lee appointed commanding general of all the armies of the Confederacy.

March 13: Bill passes Confederate Congress calling for the conscription of slaves as soldiers. Owners will be compensated, and slaves will be freed upon completion of obedient service.

April 9: Lee surrenders to Grant at Appomattox.

April 15: Lincoln assassinated.

May 4: Confederate government dissolves.

May 10: Jefferson Davis captured while running as a fugitive through Georgia and is imprisoned and remains there for two years before being released with no charges filed against him.

For Further Reading

Gabor S. Boritt, ed., *Why the Confederacy Lost*. New York: Oxford University Press, 1992. A collection of essays by Civil War historians that attempts to separate the myth from the history of why the Confederacy lost the Civil War.

Bruce Catton, *The Coming Fury: The Centennial History of the Civil War*. Garden City, NY: Doubleday, 1961. First of a multivolume history covering the events leading up to the war.

———, *Terrible Swift Sword: The Centennial History of the Civil War* Garden City, NY: Doubleday, 1963. Second of a multivolume history of the war covering the start of the war through Antietam.

———, *Never Call Retreat: The Centennial History of the Civil War*. Garden City, NY: Doubleday, 1965. Last of a multivolume history of the war covering 1863 through Appomattox.

Gary W. Gallagher, *The Confederate War*. Cambridge, MA: Harvard University Press, 1997. Examines the Confederate experience by showing how the military and the home front responded to the war and its hardships.

Mark Grimsley and Brooks D. Simpson, eds., *The Collapse of the Confederacy*. Lincoln: University of Nebraska Press, 2001. A collection of essays that explores how expectations, strategy, military performance, and nationalism affected the Confederacy during the final months of the war.

Stephen B. Oates, *The Approaching Fury: Voices of the Storm, 1820–1861*. New York: HarperCollins, 1997. First person monologues told from the viewpoints of the key players in the coming of the Civil War. Constructed from actual speeches; not factual, but entertaining.

William N. Still Jr., *The Confederate Navy: The Ships, Men and Organization, 1861–1865*. London: Conway Maritime, 1997. A richly illustrated volume detailing the history of the navy of the South.

Wiley Sword, *Southern Invincibility: A History of the Confederate Heart.* New York: St. Martin's, 1999. A view of morale among Confederate civilians and soldiers.

Craig L. Symonds, *American Heritage History of the Battle of Gettysburg.* New York: HarperCollins, 2001. An informative and vivid pictorial history of the pivotal battle.

Charles H. Wesley and Patricia W. Romero, *Afro-Americans in the Civil War.* Cornwells Heights, PA: Publishers Agency, 1978. Illustrated volume of the life of blacks in both the North and the South during the war.

C. Vann Woodward, ed., *Mary Chesnut's Civil War.* New Haven: Yale University, 1983. A collection of journal entries by a prominent South Carolina socialite provide insight into the Southern home front during the war.

Steven E. Woodworth, ed., *The Loyal, True, and Brave: America's Civil War Soldiers.* Wilmington, DE: Scholarly Research, 2002. Collection of anecdotes and essays detailing various aspects of military life during the Civil War, including enlistment, battle, medicine, imprisonment, and camp life.

Works Consulted

Books

Ralph Andreano, ed., *Economic Impact of the American Civil War.* Cambridge, MA: Schenkman, 1967. A collection of essays by noted economists that explore the various financial issues surrounding the war.

Stephen V. Ash, *When the Yankees Came: Conflict and Chaos in the Deep South, 1861–1865.* Chapel Hill: University of North Carolina Press, 1995. Explores the reaction of Southerners living under Union occupation and how it disrupted their lives.

Roy P. Basler, ed., *The Collected Works of Abraham Lincoln,* vol. 4. New Brunswick, NJ: Rutgers University Press, 1953. Part of a multivolume set of Lincoln's speeches and letters; this volume covers 1860–1861.

Richard E. Berringer, Herman Hattaway, Archer Jones, and William N. Still Jr., *Why the South Lost.* Athens: University of Georgia Press, 1986. Explores the reasons for Confederate defeat, focusing on morale and nationalism.

Robert C. Black, *The Railroads of the Confederacy.* Chapel Hill: University of North Carolina Press, 1952. A study of the railroad network of the South and the role it played in the Civil War.

Erik Bruun and Jay Crosby, eds., *Our Nation's Archive: The History of the United States in Documents.* New York: Black Dog & Leventhal, 1999. Extensive reference collection of important American documents from colonial times to the impeachment acquittal of President William Jefferson Clinton.

Thomas B. Buell, *The Warrior Generals: Combat Leadership in the Civil War.* New York: Crown, 1997. Profile of three pairs of generals and how leadership impacted the outcome of the war: Ulysses Grant and Robert E. Lee; George Thomas and John Bell Hood; and Francis Barlow and John Gordon.

Victoria E. Bynum, *The Free State of Jones: Mississippi's Longest Civil War.* Chapel Hill: University of North Carolina Press, 2001. Detailed account of a group of Union loyalists living in the Deep South and their battles with the Confederate army.

Duncan Andrew Campbell, *English Public Opinion and the American Civil War.* Woodbridge, Suffolk, UK: Boydell, 2003. A comprehensive study of political and social attitudes in England at the time of the Civil War.

Thomas L. Connelly and Archer Jones, *The Politics of Command: Factions and Ideas in the Confederate Strategy.* Baton Rouge: Louisiana State University Press, 1973. Details the evolution of Confederate military strategy and the roles commanders played in developing it.

E. Merton Coulter, *The Confederate States of America, 1861–1865.* Baton Rouge: Louisiana State University Press, 1950. An account of the military, political, and social aspects of the Confederacy.

Horace Herndon Cunningham, *Doctors in Gray: The Confederate Medical Service.* Baton Rouge: Louisiana State University Press, 1958. Details the structure and work of the Confederate military medical establishment.

William C. Davis, *Look Away! A History of the Confederate States of America.* New York: Free Press, 2002. Explores the history of the Confederacy in political, economic, and social aspects not generally covered in books that deal with this subject.

———, *The Union That Shaped the Confederacy: Robert Toombs and Alexander Stephens.* Lawrence: University Press of Kansas, 2001. Biography of two Georgia politicians whose friendship was near the center of events that led to the creation of the Confederacy and the prosecution of the war that ended it.

Marshall C. DeRosa, *The Confederate Constitution of 1861.* Columbia: University of Missouri Press, 1991. Critical analysis of the development and implementation of the Confederate Constitution.

David Herbert Donald, *Lincoln.* New York: Simon & Schuster, 1995. Thoroughly researched biography drawing from Lincoln's papers and those of his contemporaries.

Clement Eaton, *A History of the Southern Confederacy.* New York: Macmillan, 1954. Explores the causes of the war and how the Confederacy fought it.

Shelby Foote, *The Civil War: A Narrative: Fort Sumter to Perryville.* New York: Random House, 1958. First of an exhaustive three-volume work considered by many to be the definitive history of the American Civil War.

————, *The Civil War: A Narrative: Fredericksburg to Meridian.* New York: Random House, 1963. This second volume covers much of the second and third years of the war.

————, *The Civil War: A Narrative: Red River to Appomattox.* New York: Random House, 1974. The third and final volume covers the final year of the war and the fate of Jefferson Davis.

Douglas Southall Freeman, *Lee's Lieutenants: A Study in Command,* vol 1: *Manassas to Malvern Hill.* New York: Charles Scribner's Sons, 1942. This famous study of command in the East during the Civil War is known for its authoritative detail.

————, *Lee's Lieutenants: A Study in Command,* vol. 2: *Cedar Mountains to Chancellorsville.* New York: Charles Scribner's Sons, 1943. Volume 2 ends with the death of "Stonewall" Jackson.

Paul W. Gates, *Agriculture and the Civil War.* New York: Alfred A. Knopf, 1965. A study of the agricultural economy of the South during the war.

Herman Hattaway and Richard E. Berringer, *Jefferson Davis, Confederate President.* Lawrence: University Press of Kansas, 2002. Extensive biography of Jefferson Davis's time as president of the Confederacy.

Andrew Haughton, *Training, Tactics and Leadership in the Confederate Army of Tennessee: Seeds of Failure.* London: Frank Cass, 2000. A detailed account of the Army of Tennessee and the causes that led to its failure.

Archer Jones, *Civil War Command and Strategy.* New York: Free Press, 1992. Exploration of the strategies and tactics of the battlefield commanders of the war.

Ervin L. Jordan Jr., *Black Confederates and Afro-Yankees in Civil War Virginia.* Charlottesville: University of Virginia Press, 1995. A critical examination of the black experience in Civil War Virginia, including a look at free and enslaved blacks who were staunch Confederate supporters.

George Levy, *To Die in Chicago: Confederate Prisoners at Camp Douglas, 1862–1865.* Evanston, IL: Evanston, 1994. History of the Union prison at Camp Douglas, Illinois, illustrating the harsh conditions and punishments prisoners of war endured.

Ella Lonn, *Desertion During the Civil War.* Gloucester, MA: P. Smith, 1966. Examination of the causes and frequency of desertion in the Confederate and Union armies.

James M. McPherson, *Abraham Lincoln and the Second American Revolution.* New York: Oxford University Press, 1991. Scholarly interpretation of the Civil War as a second American Revolution in both its cause and its historical impact.

William Lee Miller, *Arguing About Slavery: The Great Battle in the United States Congress.* New York: Alfred A. Knopf, 1995. Uses congressional records and historical hindsight to reconstruct the debate over slavery during the 1830s.

Frank L. Owsley, *State Rights in the Confederacy.* Chicago: University of Chicago Press, 1925. One of the early authoritative examinations of the states' rights issue and the effect it had on the governing of the Confederacy and its prosecution of the war.

George C. Rable, *The Confederate Republic: A Revolution Against Politics.* Chapel Hill: University of North Carolina Press, 1994. This book investigates Confederate culture by focusing on the assumptions, values, and beliefs that formed the foundation of the South's political ideology.

James A. Rawley, *Turning Points in the Civil War.* Lincoln: University of Nebraska Press, 1966. An examination of several pivotal events during the Civil War that changed the fortunes of the North and the South.

Edward J. Renehan Jr., *The Secret Six: The True Tale of the Men Who Conspired with John Brown.* Columbia: University of South Carolina Press, 1997. Well-researched account of the radical abolitionist movement during the 1850s.

Thomas E. Schott, *Alexander H. Stephens of Georgia: A Biography.* Baton Rouge: Louisiana State University Press, 1988. A biography of the vice president of the Confederate States.

Stephen W. Sears, *Gettysburg.* New York: Houghton Mifflin, 2003. A detailed account of the pivotal battle that explores the tactical and logistical concerns of Union and Confederate commanders.

Philip Van Doren Stern, *When the Guns Roared: World Aspects of the Civil War.* Garden City, NY: Doubleday, 1965. Views of the American Civil War from the international perspective.

George Edgar Turner, *Victory Rode the Rails.* Indianapolis, IN: Bobbs-Merrill, 1953. Examines the strategic role of railroads in both the North and the South during the war.

Mark A. Weitz, *A Higher Duty: Desertion Among Georgia Troops During the Civil War.* Lincoln: University of Nebraska Press, 2000. An examination of the war's impact in Georgia and the Confederate soldiers who fought there.

David Williams, Teresa Crisp Williams, and David Carlson, *Plain Folk in a Rich Man's War: Class and Dissent in Confederate Georgia.*

Gainesville: University of Florida Press, 2000. Exploration of class issues in Georgia and their effect on the Confederate cause.

Brian Steel Wills, *The War Hits Home: The Civil War in Southeastern Virginia.* Charlottesville: University of Virginia Press, 2001. Explores the impact of the war on civilians living on the front lines of Virginia.

Stephen R. Wise, Lifeline of the Confederacy: Blockade Running duing the Civil War. Columbia: University of South Carolina Press, 1989. Study of Southern Blockade Running during the war.

Steven E. Woodworth, *Davis and Lee at War.* Lawrence: University Press of Kansas, 1995. A companion piece to *Jefferson Davis and His Generals: The Failure of Confederate Command in the West,* this book focuses on the role that Davis and Lee's relationship played in the Confederate war in Virginia.

———, *Jefferson Davis and His Generals: The Failure of Confederate Command in the West.* Lawrence: University Press of Kansas, 1990. An examination of the difficulties facing Confederate command in the West during the war.

———, *No Band of Brothers: Problems in the Rebel High Command.* Columbia: University of Missouri Press, 1999. Recalls the divisive conflicts between the Confederate commanders.

W. Buck Yearns, ed., *The Confederate Governors.* Athens: University of Georgia Press, 1985. Profiles of all the governors of the Confederate states.

Internet Source

United States Civil War Center, "Statistical Summary of America's Major Wars," June 13, 2001. www.cwc.lsu.edu/cwc/other/stats/warcost.htm.

Index

Picture Credits

About the Author

Richard Brownell is a writer living in New York City. In addition to his work for Lucent, he has written two stage plays that have received numerous productions around the country. He holds a bachelor of fine arts degree from New York University, where he was also recognized for senior achievement in screenwriting.